FIST OF FURY VOL 2

Photo Collection

"Fist of Fury The Chinese Connection Vol. 2", by Rick Baker
Compiled by Rick Baker. Foreword by Rick Baker
Contributors: Bruce Lee, Michael Worth, John Negron, Hector Martinez, Tsuyoshi Imai
Cover design: Tim Hollingsworth
Photographs from the EH Archives

Design & Layout, Nic Cairns, 22:22 Creative Media

Special thanks to: K.Reeve, George Tan, Ting Wai Ho, Nic Cairns,
Nick Singh, Alan Donkin, Brett Ratner.
Additional research material Wikipedia, *South Morning China Post*
Special mention to my mum who was as big a kung fu movie fans as me.
Special thanks to Sylvester (Sly) Raymond for being a good friend.

Special dedication to Chan Yuk. Thank you for the many images and moments in time you
left, of one of the greatest icons the world has even known – BRUCE LEE, 1940 – 1973

Every effort to trace the copyright holders of the illustrations and original layouts in this book.
In the event that any have been inadvertently overlooked, please contact the publishers
so that the situation can be rectified in future editions.

Please note: The photographs within these pages have been presented in their best quality format. Some original negatives had slight damage and it was decided to leave them as seen for authenticity (sometimes over exposed and slighty out of focus). Some contact sheets had light scratches due to age. Printing on a matt paper can sometimes highlight these issues, but time and care has been taken with the images used to give the reader the best quality presentation.

First published by Eastern Heroes © 2021. All Rights Reserved.
www.easternheroes.com
FIRST EDITION

ISBN: 978-1-7398519-4-1

All rights reserved. No parts of this publication may be reproduced or transmitted in any
form or by any means, graphic, electronic or mechanical, including photocopying, recording,
taping or any information storage and retrieval system, without prior written permission of the publisher.

OTHER TITLES AVAILABLE

Amazon.com • Barnes & Noble • Blackwells.co.uk • easternheroes.com

FIST OF FURY

Release date 22 March 1972 (Hong Kong)

"In the beginning the world had only flirted with martial art movies.
It was not until Bruce Lee came along that the world fell in love with them."

THE GREATEST REWARD IN LIFE
BY BRUCE LEE

A reporter asked if my son is very good at learning kung fu. Will he follow in your footsteps in martial arts? I think with fixed programs to teach martial arts, it will limit a person's development. I have already closed three martial arts training schools in the U.S. As to the children's future, better to leave them to develop freely.

Although I have taught my children martial arts. But it's given me a certain trouble. When studying in U.S. school, he always fights with school mates, hurting them and being complained about, and reported. So I taught him no more. My son's body is strong and healthy, good energy. He has the requirement to develop towards martial arts.

At age eighteen, I went to study in the U.S. At that time, I never thought of taking part in 'Western' films. And there were some worries. First, as a Chinese, how can you compete with Hollywood's big stars, especially as my English was not good. Second, no matter how much they pay me, I wouldn't do it if I have to appear on film with a long pigtail. So I would rather stay in the garage and basement to teach martial arts.

In 1964, there was a show of all the countries martial arts. I performed Wing Chun. A 20th Century Fox staff invited me to act on TV. It was to be *Son of Charlie Chan*, but later it changed to *Green Hornet*. I think the TV series was not a success because it was too simple and rough. But the character I played was well liked.

Reporters asked me about what I think of Cantonese movies? I don't know what to say because I was away from Hong Kong too long. I don't understand Hong Kong film industry. Don't know what to say.

The greatest reward in my life is not martial art, or movies, or being on TV. It is that I married a good foreign wife. She is kind, gracious, and always doing things to suit me. Even when I return home from work, she takes my shoes off for me. This is rare. Perhaps some people doubt two different countries people living together, with them in harmony. But my wife has become 'Chinaized'. She can speak some Cantonese for socialization and she has learned to cook Chinese food.

PUBLICITY SHOTS

Fist of Fury Photographic Collection Vol. 2

Fist of Fury Photographic Collection Vol. 2

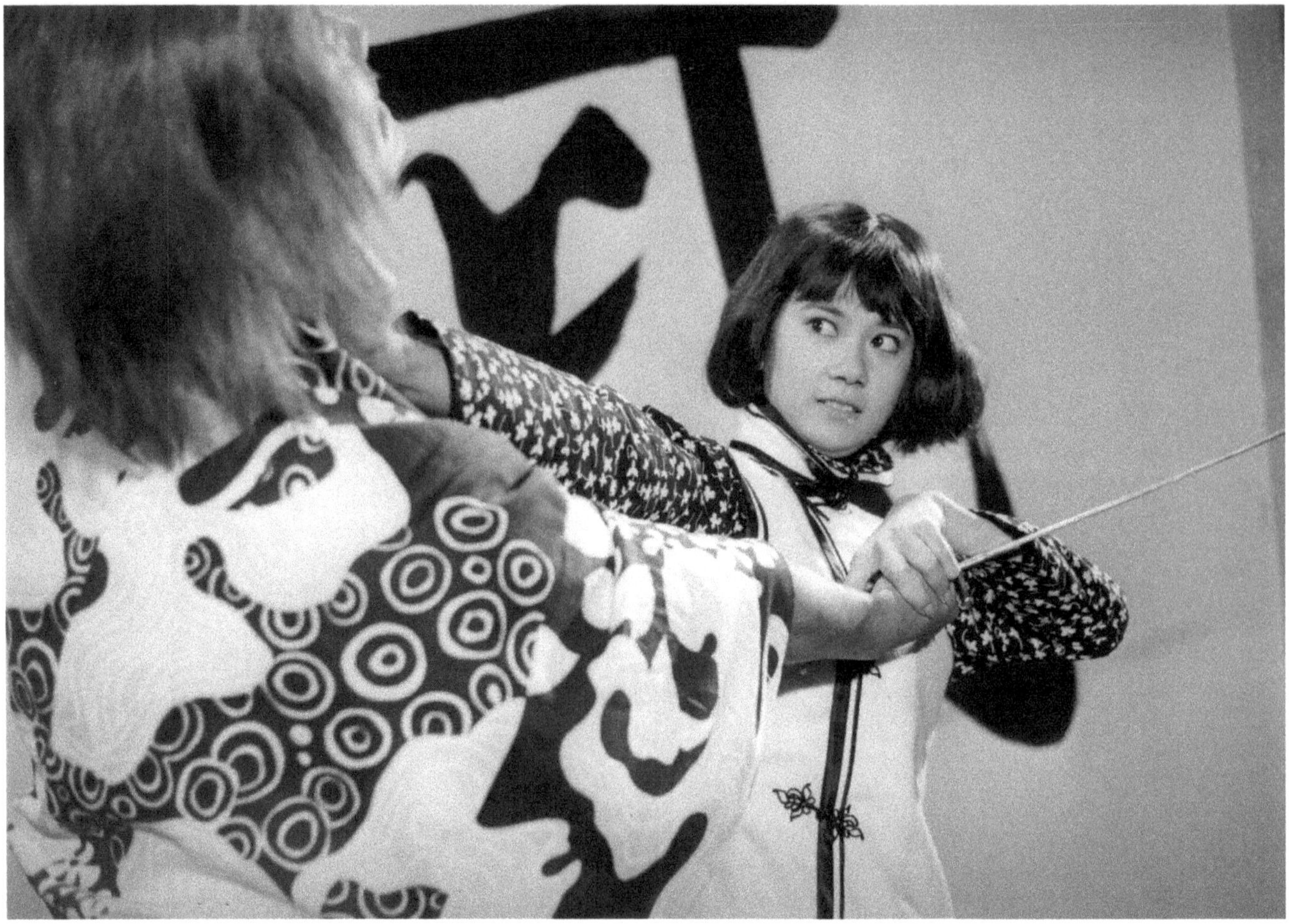

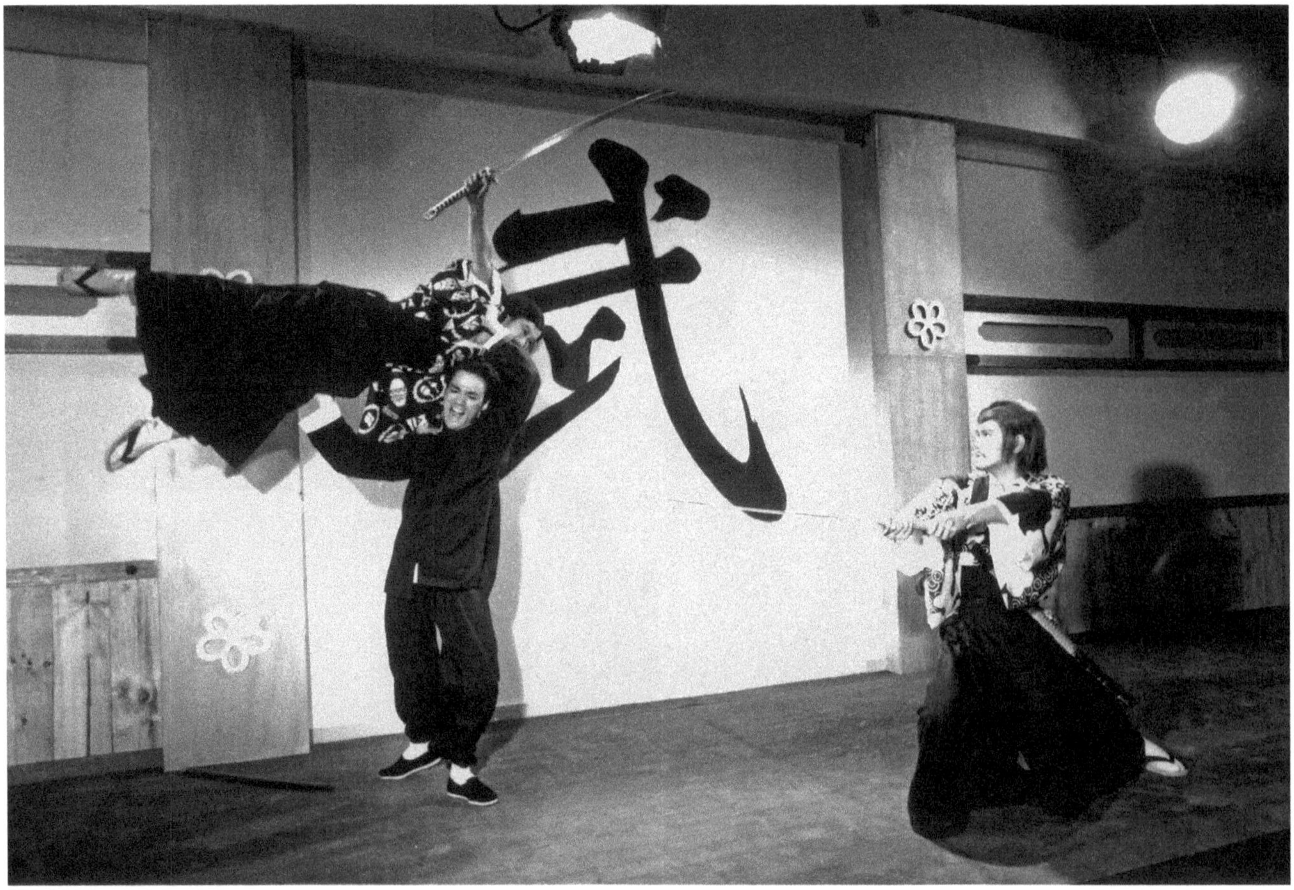
武

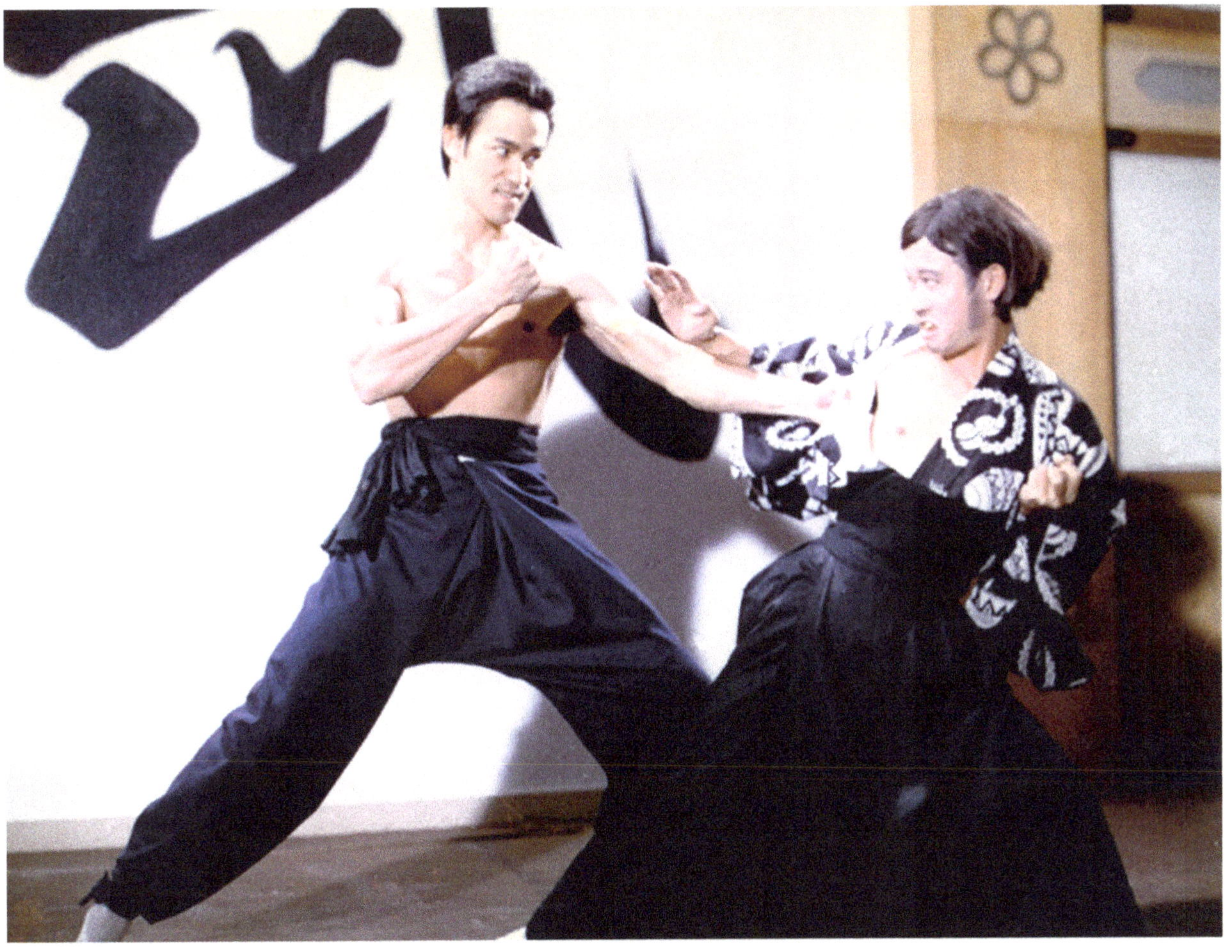

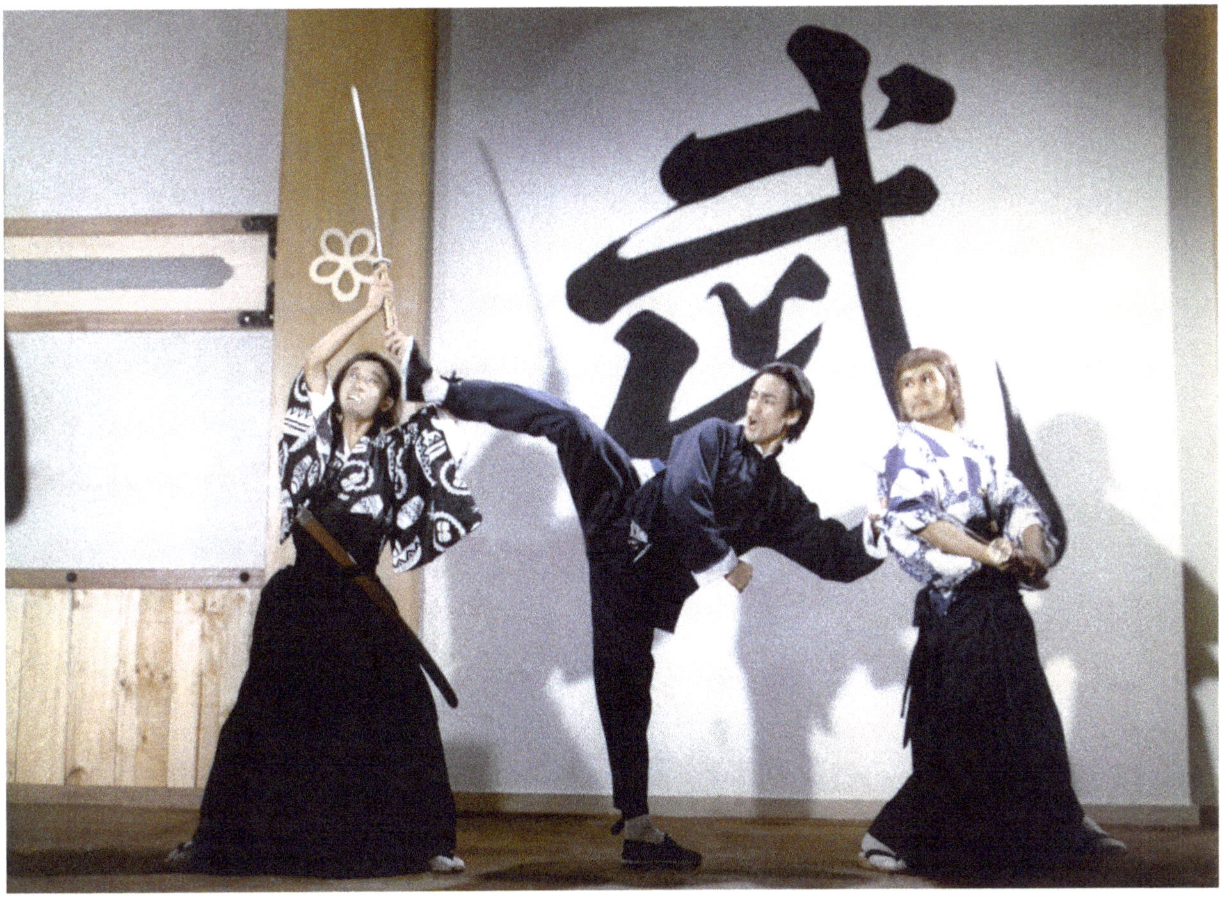

A LETTER TO BOB BAKER

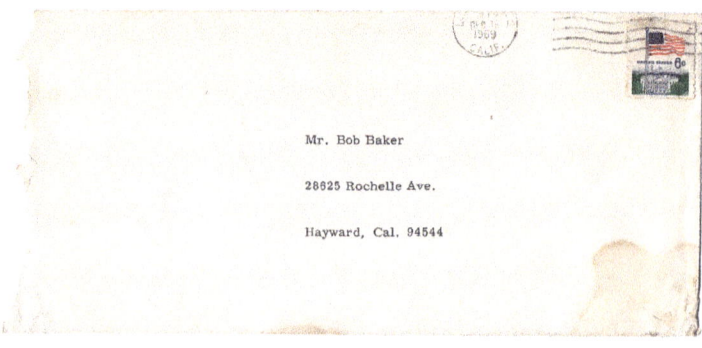

Bob,

A personal letter to thank you for bringing me the stuffs, especially the pipe and the painting. Say hello for me to Beth and family, and again thank you.

Take care

Warm Regards,

Bruce Lee

PRESS BOOK

6" DC £1.20 each

THE ART OF FURY:
THE CRAFT OF A MARTIAL ARTS CLASSIC
MICHAEL WORTH

Introduction

As a child I had seen all of Bruce Lee's completed films by the age of eleven. There was one specifically that remained my 'go to', the one where each and every showing that took place in my Bay Area backyard (back before most films were yet available on home video and only accessible in theater revivals), and that film was *Enter The Dragon* (1973). There is plenty to enjoy about *Dragon*, the assembly of soon-to-be-stars who permeate the background, The Lalo Schifrin beats, the memorable lines, the red-letter fight sequences and of course the infinite charisma of Bruce Lee. The production has its moments of effective craftsmanship but over all it is a film that survives on its energetic colorful presentations. For those who have watched it with a kung fu ravenous crowd, you know those specific moments which the film pivots around as they are met with a deafening roar of applause and shouts every time.

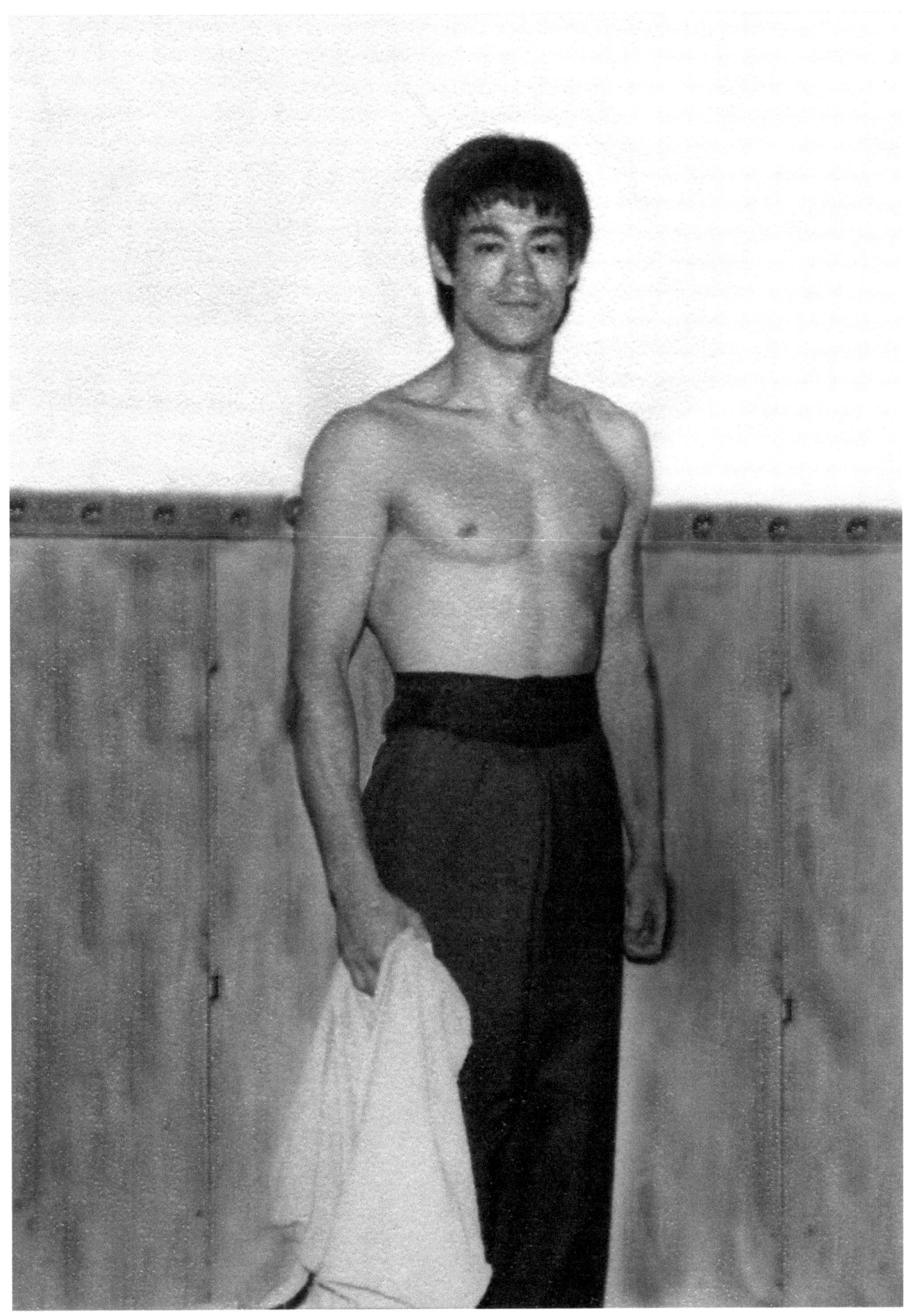

Over the years as I began to carve out my own filmmaking career, I would return to these movies often in preparation (yes, they are still very instructive to filmmakers today as you will see). I would soon find myself beginning to take particular note of *Fist of Fury* (1972), Lee's second starring role. As I observed the production less from the eye of an adrenaline junkie child and more from that of a director and choreographer, I was realizing the cinema artistry within this kung fu classic has often been overlooked (at least by me). The years have continued to open my eyes to its many achievements beyond Lee's obvious magnetism, particularly with the effort of his partners, director Lo Wei and cinematographer Chris Chen. *Fury* may never overtake the jazzy vigor of *Enter The Dragon*, but the film stands out as likely the most well constructed film of all their careers.

Volumes have been written on Bruce Lee's life and career (I probably own many of them) and there is no overstating his personal ingredient within this film's massive status and success, but it is also his support system behind the camera that we owe much to for allowing Lee's magic to flourish on this, his most captivating stage.

Director Lo Wei began as an actor during World War II working mainly in stage productions, finally making a strong impression in his debut in cinema with *Sorrows of the Forbidden City* (1948) for Yung Hwa Motion Picture Industries Limited. In the following years, through his experience as an actor on camera, he developed what I believe to be one of his strongest suits as a director: cinematic staging. That is where the actors occupy specific dynamic areas in the frame and work in relationship to the movement of the camera to convey attention, aesthetic tone and trope. This evolution can be evident through his tenure at Shaw Brothers (prior to his and Raymond Chow's exodus) between *Crocodile River* (1964), where his staging thrives on a symmetrical frame centered production and *The Golden Sword* (1969) where

his experimentation of camera space and movement had distinctly evolved. Though Lo Wei was an inconsistent man at the helm, he did showcase a certain camera-actor relationship acumen of which quite possibly no better example exists than in Fist of Fury (1972).

Wei's partner in the assembly of Fury, joining him for the second time, was cinematographer Chris Chen (the pair would do half a dozen films under the Golden Harvest banner). The duo re-teamed later with Jackie Chan on Killer Meteors (1976), Chris even re-joining Chan directing his own classic The Young Master (1980), where the cinematographer would showcase more consistently secure camera work. But it was his pairing with Wei and Lee that created some of his most thoughtful and even ethereal work as a cinematographer. Fury transcends the action to become a moody drama about struggle and bravery that inspired generations of filmmakers, martial artists and movie fans across the world.

Mise En Fury

The opening image of Fist of Fury is a powerful widescreen 2.35:1 aspect image of the Shanghai Mountains dwarfed by the ensuing rain storm. But it is in the very next frame, a high wide angle shot of the entrance to Ching Wu School, that we are given several gripping elements. It is the first image of our hero Chen Zhen ((Bruce Lee, whose name I will use when referencing the character to avoid the confusion with the cinematographer) emerging from a rickshaw dressed in the traditional mourning white as he turns from us and rushes into the gates of Ching Wu. This moment is of interest as not only does it establish immediately the setting of the historic martial arts school, but because it will coincide with the closing shot of the film. The story's concluding image is on a similar axis of the building, Leer now in a contrasting shirtless torso and black trousers, running now towards the lens (as well as his death) within the exact same access way. The movie is literally bookended by the same image of the school's admittance but with Lee entering in a state of remorse and departing in a state of furious insurrection. The observer may not consciously note this placement and staging but this effective bookending will visually encourage the aforementioned tone of this hard-hitting story.

The very next reverse shot is where Lee is revealed more fully and represents a camera move Lo Wei and Chris Chen use to effect often – but to my mind to its greatest effect within this film. As Lee approaches the lens into a medium frame he pauses in recognition of something off camera. Instead of cutting to what he is looking at, the camera lingers and then pans with Lee as he enters the building, finally settling on an 180 degree turn, the angle now over Lee to his gaze of the honouring display for his deceased teacher Hou Yunjia. This use of a non-cutting camera move to reveal an off screen element, when done well, pulls the viewer into an anticipatory state of reveal over a simple quick reverse cut. It is used again several minutes later into the film when Cheung Hei, the eulogist, is speaking at the memorial display, and while speaking about Hou he again motivates the pan to reveal the mass of Ching Wu students in the hall listening to him speak, the effect of their reveal much more prominent as a result.

Moments later in the same hall when some of the offensive Japanese led by Paul Wei's interpreter enter, the construction of the staging becomes manifold in its complexity. Utilizing the camera so that it neither muddles up actors upon actors in frame nor over stages the sequence can be difficult. But here, careful observation of the actors placements in Wei's and Chen's productions reveals a fairly conscious care to craft. In the construction of the dozen or so wide shots of the group, Lee in his white suit is often positioned in a central line between the Japanese and the Chinese Ching Wu men. The attention of the observer's eye is drawn to him through the gauntlet of darker dressed actors, the man who is quite literally standing between the Ching Wu and the Japanese invaders.

Another example of Wei's framing to draw special focus to Lee is in one of the more iconic moments of *FOF*: Lee's dismantling of the "No Dogs and Chinese" sign - the moment he transforms into the champion of the locals. Once Lee has confronted the park guard in several cuts to build the tension, a wide shot then brings in Yuen Wah (as a local Japanese) and his cohort from the left side of camera. As they approach Lee, several citizen extras dressed in white and black align each side of the frame uniformly creating, along with the stone

posts, an optical physical pointer towards Lee directly between. Wei's other films in this period including *The Hurricane* (1972) and *The Invincible Eight* (1971) gave him the opportunity and the exercise of working from much more colorful wardrobe and set design, often using them in poignant arrangement of sequences to draw the viewer's eye. With *Fury*, Wei's color tones were more dark with black, white and grays so the visual grouping would often revolve around more contrasting arrangements coupled with camera and actor placement.

Wei's use of a roving camera over simple cuts to reveal information in frame is not solely notable in the collaborations with Chen. Some of Wei's output at Shaw Brothers showcases a more elevated eye to construction than his reputation as a dog-race obsessed director may suggest. The sequence in *Dragon Swamp* (1969), shot with Shaw Brothers cinematographer Wu Cho-hua, where Cheng Pei-pei enters the tavern and is followed in by a series of various robbers is an effective use of dolly tracks and pans to create an elevated moment of ambush. Each character enters on a dolly move, their various end points of the shot creating a visual relationship with Pei-pei's character Fan Ying within the tavern. The longer takes and camera movement over simple master shot/close-up cutting builds both tension and dynamic visuals prior to the fight. Lee's dojo fight in *Fury* follows a similar rhythm; a ballet of slow dolly shots before the tango.

The now cliché zoom shot that we associate with the kung fu cinema of the 1970s is blissfully underused in this film, relying mainly on prime lenses to achieve the visuals. Chang Cheh and the Shaw Bros pool of directors would hone and use the zoom often, helping them maneuver through cuts within the action, but by the late 1970s it was ubiquitous throughout even non-action scenes. (Though some ,like director Lau Kar-leung, have created some masterful uses of it in films like *Return to the 36th Chamber of Shaolin* (1980) as well.) There are some notable uses of it in *Fury* including the slower zoom into Lee's face as he overhears the conspirators in the kitchen as well as one of the very last shots of the film, the snap zoom to the firing squad waiting outside for Lee. Another notable moment of several uses in *Fury* are in the "No Dogs or Chinese" sequence where Lee defeats Yuen Wah and his men. The final two knock out techniques (a punch and a jump kick) to the two opponents are both punctuated with a snap zoom into Lee's face. The opposite is

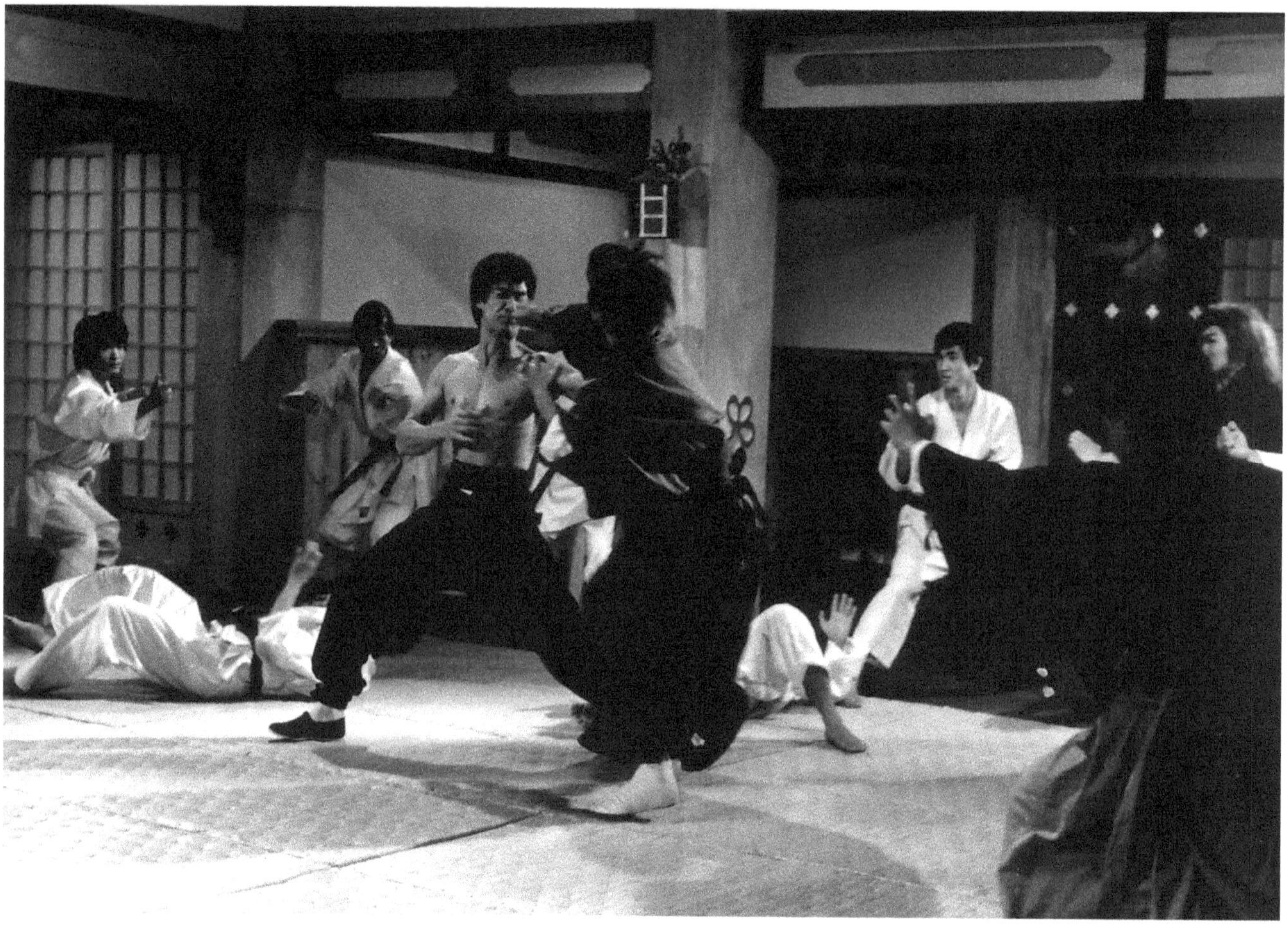

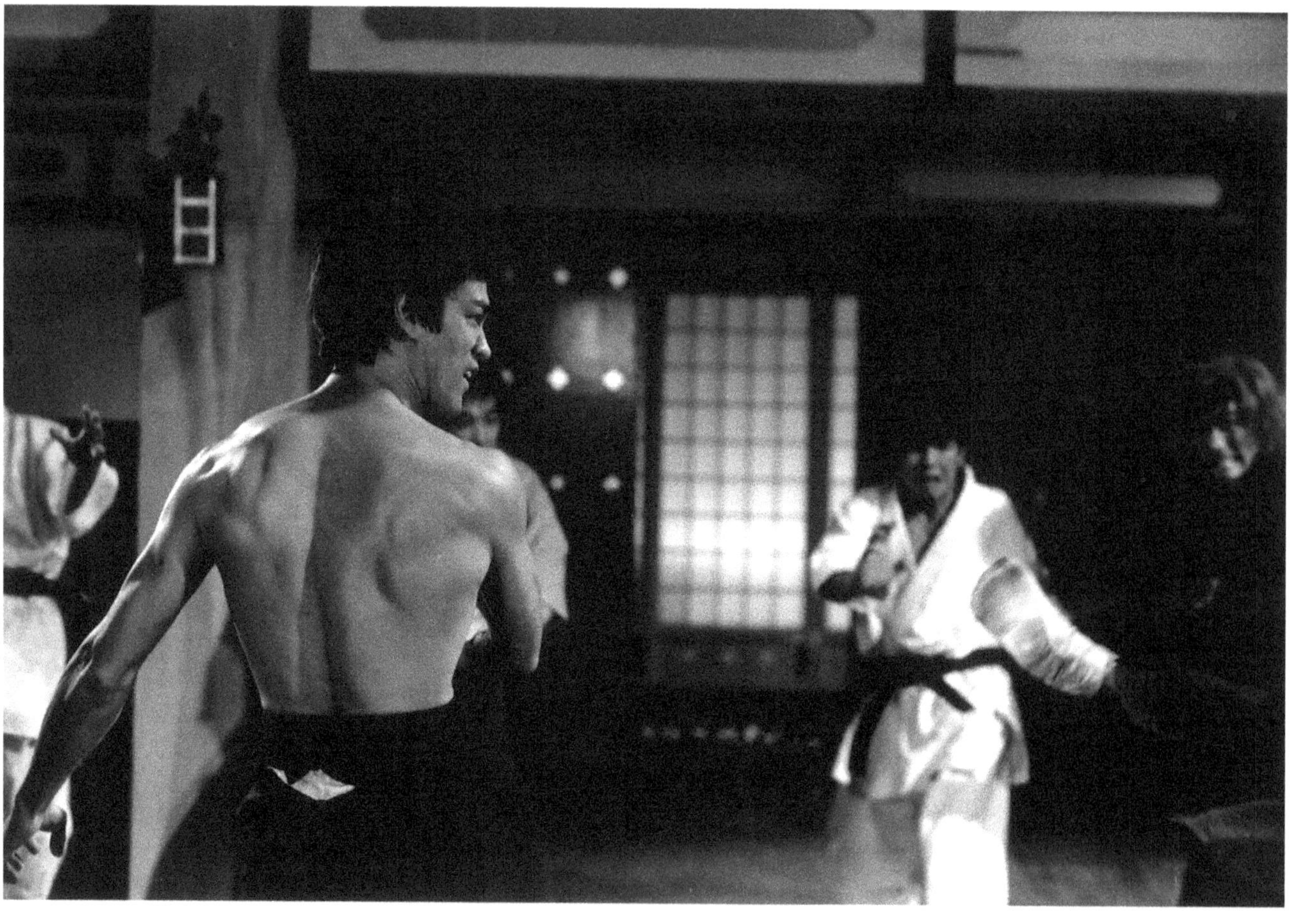

done when the notorious "Sick Men of Asia" is revealed to the Japanese in their dojo. Rather than accentuating Lee, there is a snap into Yoshida's face to emphasize the impact of the reaction to the bold statement of the young Chinese fighter.

For the most part, each use of the zoom here justifies a certain dynamic that may not have worked as well with a lens change. Wei and Chen also utilized it in a similar punctuation to both *The Big Boss* and *Fury* to enclose their stories. In *Boss* as Lee withdraws his fingers from Han's chest and punches him to the ground, the camera from a starting long wide shot snaps tighter into Lee delivering various overkill shots in his rage. Several shots later, the shot reverses and zooms back out in conjunction with Lee's collapsing in exhaustion on top of Han's body, the fight finally at a close. In the end of *Fury* as Chen steps from Ching Wu School and pauses, the camera then reverses and punches quickly into the firing squad awaiting, signifying the last act of defiance into martyrdom. The technique of the zoom can often be a lazy form of lens change (wide to tight or tight to wide) but in *Fury*, Wei's use here often plays more intelligently for visual emphasis.

Lens placement within a scene and around actors can provide elements of narrative information without exposition. When we meet the story's villain Suzuki (Hashimoto Riki) for instance, it is in low wide angle shot as he brings his fist down on the table in front of us. Once he stands and moves into the depth of the shot at the doorway the move reveals a couple other players in the room, all lower than him in the frame. The reverse cut is a medium-wide shot opening up even more characters in the room with Suzuki now in a dominant close up but remaining eerily out of focus as his gaze wanders. The following shot of Suzuki is low and menacing, completing a trilogy of images to introduce him in a purely aggressive and governing fashion as well as the meticulous unveiling of his minions. It's not much, but it creates our antagonist's relationship to the other characters and his presence on screen.

Lo Wei chose to follow a more traditional use of a high angle or mid angle lens through much of the action. There was a trending style within action choreography to rely on the powerful low shot that Shaw Brothers' legend Chang Cheh considered a 'warm' choice over the more traditional 'colder' high angle shots of the 1950s and 1960s. This would be one of many creative exchanges the Shaw filmmakers learned working with the Japanese technicians from Toho, Daiei, etc. Cheh was one to ride and expand on the new wave cinema experimentation. In his 1967 film *The Assassin* with Jimmy Wang Yu, Cheh took this approach even further and experimented with a far more frequent use of static low angles to capture

most of the film's action. Though Wei and Chen would not abandon all the Japanese influenced camera work for *Fury*. In fact Lee himself on many levels was inspired by the performance from one of his own favorite Japanese films; Tatsuya Nakadai in *Sword of Doom* (1966). Exploring that film's influence and similarity to *Fury* could be an essay in itself.

Fighting Focus

Most familiar with Shaw Brothers productions will note an often stylized slick and crafted look to the productions and action that for Wei, Chen and Lee's first film *The Big Boss* was out of reach. Location shooting on a budget can force the filmmaker into areas of creativity relying less on structured set ups and more on spontaneous ingenuity. The term constructive editing refers to sequences built on the individual shots of a sequence over the longer/wider takes to give us a broader picture of a scene. This was used both in early Chinese and Soviet cinema (think Eisenstein) and helped many a non-martial artist enjoy a cinema make over into a more heroic figure. The very influential *The Chinese Boxer*, which I find to be an entertaining film on so many levels, constructs much of its action utilizing this approach. On locations like *The Big Boss*, a rarer circumstance for Shaw's mostly in studio productions (Though Chang Cheh's 1966 *Tiger Boy* is a notable exception to this), the use of constructive editing was more common. But Lee was one who both wanted to showcase his skills in longer wide takes and would be granted the opportunity more notably in *Fist of Fury* while shooting on their Golden Harvest studio lot.

Lee's initial fight at the dojo (one of the most entertaining and creative fight scenes in Lee's career, in my opinion) as he prepares to fight his opponents all at once is a prime example. There begins a careful build up while Lee removes his shirt, Wei cutting back and forth between medium shots of Lee preparing himself and the Japanese students nervously deciding on an attack. Then the first technique is caught by an overhead wide shot that follows through eight kicks executed in one static shot, demonstrating Lee's speed and skill without trick. After a quick reaction shot to Yoshida (Fung Ngai) Wei and Chen create a short

tracking shot again following Lee from right to left as he goes through a series of seven opponents. Lee's action choreography in this, though linear in direction, is circular in movement as Lee turns and twists to throw and hit his opponents, creating more dimensional movement. This is defining it somewhat from the choreography of Han Ying Chieh and one can watch the Japanese attack on the Ching Wu school utilizing a similar camera dolly with more linear choreography to note the difference.

After a reaction shot of Cory Yuen hitting a beam, we then get one more seven second static shot of Lee going through one man per second. The middle tracking shot is an interesting one with parallels to one in *The Sword of Doom* (1966). The famous ambush sequence in the film involves a long singular tracking shot as Nakadai goes through his enemies, following a linear path with circular movement of attack and defense. But it would be this analytical editing style which hid little from the viewer that made this first fight sequence in the film command attention. These long well crafted and energetic shots helped usher in a new bar for action cinema to aspire to.

Lo Wei's use of slow motion would be in economical and thoughtful use throughout the film. High speed shooting (in effect, slow motion playback) became wildly popular with Peckinpah in his westerns (Akira Kurosawa's genius made use of it as far back as Seven Samurai in 1955) and could be often overused to the point of exhausting its effect but the inclusion of it here is subtle and expertly applied. Its first instance comes when Lee confronts Han Ying-chieh and Huang Chung-hsin who have poisoned his teacher. This moodily lit sequence in the kitchen involves Lee leaping into an atypical use of props via kicking the men from the table top and engaging Huang in a quick back and forth. Wei offers up a close up as Lee chambers his punch and then in a bold two shot of the men, the frame rate now slowed down, Lee lands the punch in this impressive reality shift. This punch by all intents and purposes is the titular Fist of Fury that now has crossed the line of no return, killing its first man. The slowed down motion and its alteration in tone and visual experience signifies to us this crucial moment. The sound has transformed as well, the diegetic noise now replaced by what can only be described as some otherworldly reverberations. There is also a shift to Lee's performance as well, as here is where the dark crazed reaper begins, his only calming moments

generally from Nora Miao's presence. The next use of slow motion interestingly enough is the death of the cook's brother, Yoshida (Fung Ngai) in the final act.

When Lee faces Yoshida this second time at the climax, both men are paused in a moment of contemplative combat and we have a beautiful frame that summarizes the martial arts theme of the movie: Japanese Karate vs Chinese Gung Fu. On the left side of screen (generally reserved for your villain) Yoshida holds his sword in ready, bathed in a colder blue light while on the heroic right side of frame, Lee is holding a much more representative posture of gung fu, a warm light juxtaposed behind his head. This freeze frame of preparation indicates so much of the feud that has taken place and is a beautifully composed example of Wei's willingness to let the wider frame play out in his action with Lee. The sequence of slow motion follows as the sword comes down through the Japanese man's back and Lee finishes him off once again with the fist that killed his brother.

Dolly shots were a favorite of Wei's as indicated. Before a steady cam was available to the world at large (though was only a couple years away) the moving dolly was one way the new wave directors of Wei's time were adding kinetic dimension to their action and drama. As mentioned earlier, Wei's use of the 180 degree cameras pan often involved some dolly movement, but in the action sequences of *Fury* it serves both a beautiful uninterrupted realignment of camera for a series of new techniques or as a useful tool of tension within the action. In Lee's first fight scene in the dojo as the Japanese (Peter Chan) moves slowly to take on Lee, the camera dollies with him from the right to the left where he meets Lee, revealed at the end of the move. Lee is now positioned high on the left, looking dominant above Chan as he then evades a punch and flips him. The following shot essentially reverses the direction, starting now on Lee as he moves slowly, deeper into the dojo towards Chan. As the camera move nears its end arranging them into a wide two shot, Chan charges and Lee fires off a roundhouse continuing into a spin kick that at the tail end, the other Japanese (Max Lee) enters and is struck. This leads to a high shot of Max commanding the students to surround Lee and with that, we cut to an even higher wide shot as the human circle is formed.

This sequence is a powerful one in its use of the camera and timing. The slow dolly heightens the build up to come, slow dancing with Lee and Chan as one moves out and then the other moves in. Then in the final kick, Max's sudden entrance at the tail end of the kick gives the impression Lee saw something we didn't, heightening his ability. On the 'surround' command, it plays very 'musically' as we have just gone through these paced beats of combat that end in a crescendo as all move into position for the coming chorus assault. This rhythm continues as the all-on-one assault ends with Lee grabbing his nunchaku, pausing the rapid action with another 'song' while he spins them. This was the most notable introduction of the weapon into cinema and this moment acquaints us with their power before Cory Yuen and the others rush in to discover it for themselves. The shot of Lee is one of the lowest angles of him in the sequence (the same shot is used at the end of the sequence with a tighter lens change when he drops the nunchakus) and gives Lee a powerful and dominant position in frame.

Lee's assault on the dojo in the climax is a mix of various camera techniques and staging that Wei has been using throughout the film but in a newly structured way, specifically in the Bob Baker fight which becomes the highlight. After Lee has dispatched the handful of body guards in the courtyard, there is a moment of pause as the Russian and the Chinese avenger lock eyes. We go to a wide shot as Baker slowly unbuttons his jacket and then follows one of Wei's characteristic near 180 degree camera pan to follow Baker into a classic confrontational two shot that reveals Lee waiting on the left side of frame. There is a series of medium cuts of the men looking at each other (later replicated by Lee with Norris in *Way of the Dragon*, 1972) before the start of the first set of choreography is again caught in a wide shot. This series of choreography and beats of pause is clearly Lee's influence from the samurai films and is notably different again from Han Ying-cheih's pacing and techniques up to this point in his career. (Lo Wei's *A Man Called Tiger* (1973) was intended for Lee, but Jimmy Wang Yu, who did not come close to the same athleticism or skill, took over the role, and in the sequence in the abandoned warehouse for instance where Han and Jimmy square off to fight, Han borrows some clear rhythms and techniques from Lee's playbook that would not exist in Han's earlier films, with King Hu in example.)

The Baker fight continues to exhibit some wide shots alternating with medium size close ups, low and overhead shots as well as a few dutch angles that visually give this fight sequence a unique feel separating it from the others in the film. The staging of the men along with the rhythm of the pause-fight-pause give this a much more samurai-influenced (even spaghetti western) tempo to the action. Towards the climax of the scene, there are a series of cuts between the men, each succeeding one getting closer and closer to their eyes. Then after a snap zoom into Suzuki's face we cut back to a wide shot of the two men. Once they move we realize we are in slow motion, a technique served well in *The Seven Samurai*, as Lee launches a kick to Baker's head. The slow motion continues through several shots until just before the final throat kill shot where we go back to twenty four frames, giving the last shot even more impact.

Martial Metaphor

There are many ways to tell a story and to indicate emotion and relationships in a film. Dialogue is the most common route but through careful constructed visuals, the filmmaker can communicate ideas that don't require the conscious mind to decipher. The use of lighting, camera angles, props and the mise en scene (fancy word for staging of actors in relationship to the lens) are the director's tools to color the tone of his script. *Fury* holds many examples of this, some we have noted, and they help raise this film from a point of cinema craft to one of the best in Wei's and Lee's career.

This film has within its hyper vengeful premise a love story with Lee and Nora Miao. It does not use up much narrative time but is established in a couple of key scenes: in Ching Wu School and in the graveyard. What is notable about these scenes where their ultimately doomed relationship is expressed is not the words but rather the elements. In the first scene, taking place right before Lee discovers the conspiracy that killed his master, is at the base of a Hou Yunjia's memorial display. What may seem a strange place to express a romantic relationship becomes clear when their next and last moment of intimacy is in the same teacher's graveyard. Is this the director in some way through his location choice expressing the doomed relationship? Or maybe the overseeing force of the famed instructor bringing them together? Interestingly, both scenes are balanced out by another reoccurring element: fire. The flame of the candle in the Ching Wu school and the flame of Lee's cooking fire are both prominently featured, potentially showing the resistance to the death surrounding them or implicating the presence of Ho Yunjia or their love within the fire.

Another notable theme used throughout the film are the signs used by both sides of the fight to combat and posture to each other. Considering the language barrier that exists between the warring clans, the use of a symbol or gesture to communicate their advances is not a surprise. The first most obvious one is

the "Sick Men of Asia" plaque delivered to Ching Wu by the Japanese and then ceremoniously stuffed back down the Japanese's throat. These messages and symbols, direct or indirect, permeate the movie in a back and forth game of chess. The next gesture is more a macro communication to the community involving the "No Dogs or Chinese" sign that once again Lee will physically destroy, one of the other more iconic moments in the film. So Lee himself is sending his own messages back to them in both the destroying of their own signs as well as in his hanging the dead bodies from the street lamp posts. The two Japanese and the Chinese interpreter (Paul Wei) are hung from these posts as human indicators of Lee's success against them. Lee will also smash a smaller sign hanging in the dojo as he leaves the initial fight early in the film. This idea of language being used and even destroyed through means other than spoken language is another interesting way of communicating narrative and intention in the story.

After *Fury*, Lee would make his directorial debut with *Way of the Dragon* and along with his filmed sequences for *Game of Death* (1972), he would would convince another Shaw Brothers trained technician to come over to Golden Harvest, Japanese cinematographer Nishimoto Tadashi. Nishimoto was no slouch, not only had he filmed the anamorphic horror classic in Japan, *Black Cat Mansion* (1958) but would become a notable cameraman at the Shaws', shooting the King Hu masterpiece, *Come Drink With Me* (1966). And though Nishimoto was a finely trained cameraman and Lee a promising director, it was Chris Chen who in my opinion gave Lee some of his most visual and impactful sequences specifically in *Fury* along with Lo Wei clearly on the top of his game. This trio of filmmakers would create one of the most influential and important martial arts films that should sit alongside King Hu's *Touch of Zen* and Kurosawa's *Seven Samurai* as a truly genre transcending film. Though as a youngster obsessed with Lee's cavern battle on Han's island, I have learned to deepen my appreciation for the cinematic experience of *Fist of Fury* and all its intricate components that still marvels my eleven year old self today.

THE INTERPRETER

40   *Fist of Fury* Photographic Collection Vol. 2

EVERYBODY WAS KUNG FU FIGHTING
JOHN NEGRON

The year is 1971, John Negron is a wee lad of eleven years old and the cinemas in the U.S. were approaching a brand-new genre like never seen before. It was to be labelled the kung fu craze and soon everybody would be kung fu fighting.

This craze would grip us like a jumping side kick to the head and not let go for many years to come. A young man named Bruce Lee would lead us into this soon to become cult fascination with chop socky as the media would refer to it and the rest is history. So, looking back I can remember watching Shaw Brothers *Five Fingers of Death* aka *King Boxer* with a young star named Lo Lieh which was the first to break the ice and WOW, did the ice break! Words cannot describe the excitement that American audiences were experiencing. The first time

we had ever witnessed a film like this. We had never seen anything like what was about to happen like jumping and fighting five feet in the air, poking out eyes, the gore, the punching, kicking just glued us to the screen. Now fast forward to 1972, I hear the ad like it was just yesterday on the radio and TV they say he is "unstoppable!, unbelievable!, unbeatable!", The master of karate kung fu is back with *The Chinese Connection*, aka *Fists of Fury*. The rest is of course a phenomenon that cannot be explained if you didn't live it at the time. To witness Bruce Lee on the screen while he was still alive was just an incredible experience that only movie goers of that day could describe. There were to be many more come along but the man with the screams and lightning-fast feet and hands was to set the stage. I know many fans and collectors have seen *Chinese Connection* countless times on TV, VHS, and DVD etc...BUT to see it on the big screen back in 1972 it's an experience that can't be forgotten or described. I will never forget sitting in the theatre and watching the movies countless times and no one put us out sitting through double and triple features for less than US $3.00. We sneaked in 40-oz bottles of beer in brown paper bags, snacks for the munchies, and the little funny rolled cigarettes. Now mix in a rowdy crowd that came to

see the guy from *Fists of Fury* aka *The Big Boss* and we were ready to be entertained. No REALLY entertained!. By this time the secret was out this was the guy that played Kato on *The Green Hornet* and the movie goers were ready to see BRUCE LEE an boy did we see him. It was as if he jumped off the screen!! Larger than life, his persona, the aura, the body, the screams, the fury that came off the screen, I call it INTENSITY. The audience in New York was a mixed one and here he was a Chinese guy representing the minority against injustice from the Japanese, so the audience went CRAZY!! I mean absolutely NUTS!! Picture this if you will, people standing up cheering, screaming at Bruce to kick ass, you couldn't even hear the movie because everyone was on their feet cheering Bruce on to stand up against the bullies of the school and their race. I will never forget watching the screen and not being able to blink because I did not want to miss anything. The scene that did it that day back in 1972 was when Bruce walked into the dojo and totally demolished the Japanese school like a one-man terminator and then for the first time, we witnessed the nunchaku or nunchakus as we used to call them, everybody was up on their feet screaming and yelling at the screen!! What the heck kind of weapon was this we said to ourselves?

Man, I want to swing these! We went out the movie doing screams jumping and kicking at each with all the sounds effects and guess what we were kung fu experts emulating the characters on the screen, completely excited at what we saw all the way home. Now time to make those 'Chuks he had in the film so we thought we made them from a broom stick cut in two equal pieces, chain and or a rope back then and now to swing them like Bruce and boy did we swing we beat up our elbows put knots on the back of our heads and made the swishing sound just like in the movie trying to master them just like Bruce did and impersonate our hero that we witnessed on the screen. Well, that scene was forty-nine years ago and it made such an impression on me that to this day I still get just as excited watching that film that I did back in 1972. And so, 1972 brought us Bruce Lee in *Chinese Connection* and we couldn't wait to see what was next because Bruce Lee and kung fu mania was here to stay. Our hero had arrived like nothing we had ever seen before.

Fist of Fury Photographic Collection Vol. 2

COLLECTION OF FURY
HECTOR MARTINEZ

Growing up during the summer of 1973 was a revelation! Never did I expect that what I would experience in 1973 would stay with me for 48 years into 2021. I'm not even talking about parties, girls and fashion (although they too are memorable) it's much more important than that, I'm talking about the BRUCE LEE EXPLOSION! Sure we had Jimmy Wang Yu, Angela Mao, David Chiang and Ti Lung but when the Bruce Lee films hit our neighbourhood grindhouse theatres the impact was twice as hard and twice as loud as a nuclear explosion!

The first time I saw Bruce Lee was in a double bill consisting of *Fists of Fury* (*Big Boss*) and *Chinese Connection* (*Fist of Fury*). Of course came later *Enter* then *Way* but the one that to me embodied the totality of Bruce Lee was *Chinese Connection*!

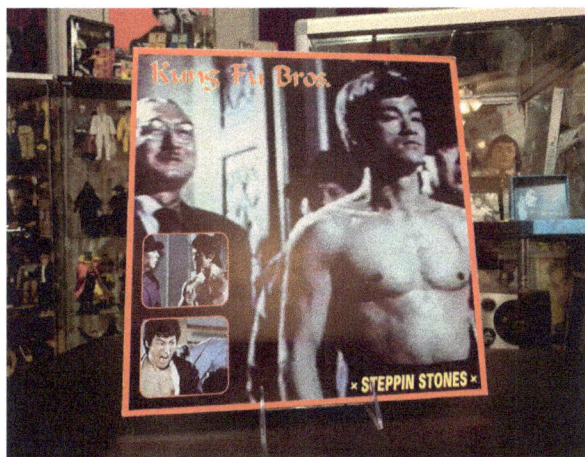

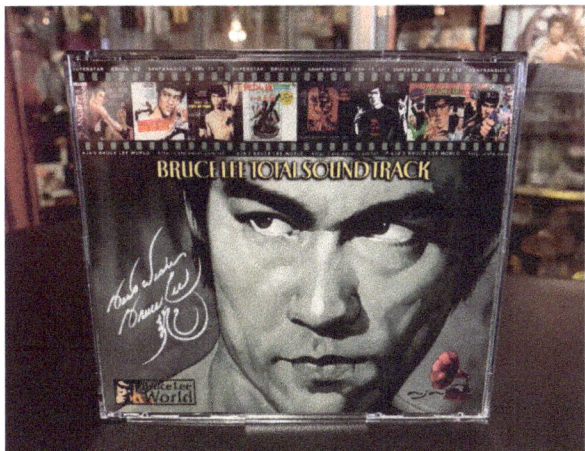

Let's start with the U.S. theatrical poster and lobby cards: I remember standing in front of the movie theatre waiting for my turn to be re-introduced to Bruce Lee (saw him for the first time in 1966 on the *Green Hornet* series) and when I took a glimpse of the poster and the lobby cards that were neatly displayed in the front of the theatre little did I know that I'd be writing about them for *Eastern Heroes* magazine in 2021. I mean the poster was hypnotic, the four purple images of Bruce in flight from the classic and thrilling climax of the film was enough to give me tachycardia lol! I'll never forget seeing the heading "Unstoppable!, Unbelievable!, Unbeatable!"

I was convinced that not only was I in for a treat but that I was going to need to learn about Asian culture because from that moment forwards I was going to be half Asian and half Hispanic! Bruce Lee was absolutely and prophetically on point when he told Pierre Burton back in 1971 that "Things of Chinese will be interesting for the next few years."

52   *Fist of Fury* Photographic Collection Vol. 2

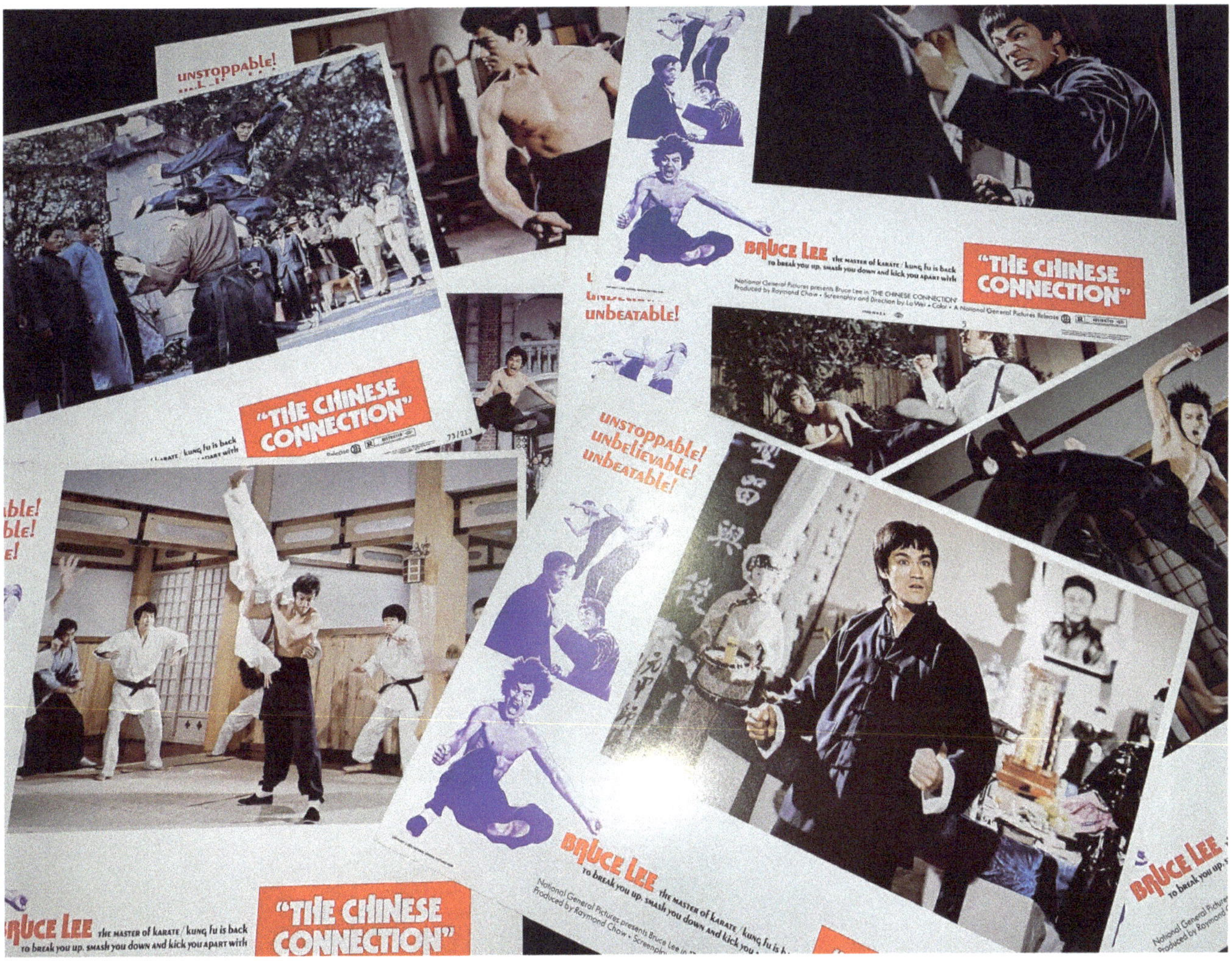

unstoppable!
"THE CHINESE CONNECTION"
BRUCE LEE the master of karate / kung fu is back
unstoppable! unbelievable! unbeatable!
"THE CHINESE CONNECTION"

unstoppable! unbelievable! unbeatable!
BRUCE LEE
"THE CHINESE CONNECTION"
National General Pictures presents Bruce Lee in "THE CHINESE CONNECTION"
Produced by Raymond Chow • Screenplay and Direction by Lo Wei • Color • A National General Pictures Release
73/213
unstoppable! unbelievable! unbeatable!
BRUCE LEE
to break you up, smash you down
"THE CHINESE CONNECTION"
National General Pictures presents Bruce Lee in "THE CHINESE CONNECTION"
Produced by Raymond Chow • Screenplay and Direction by Lo Wei • Color • A National General Pictures Release
73/213

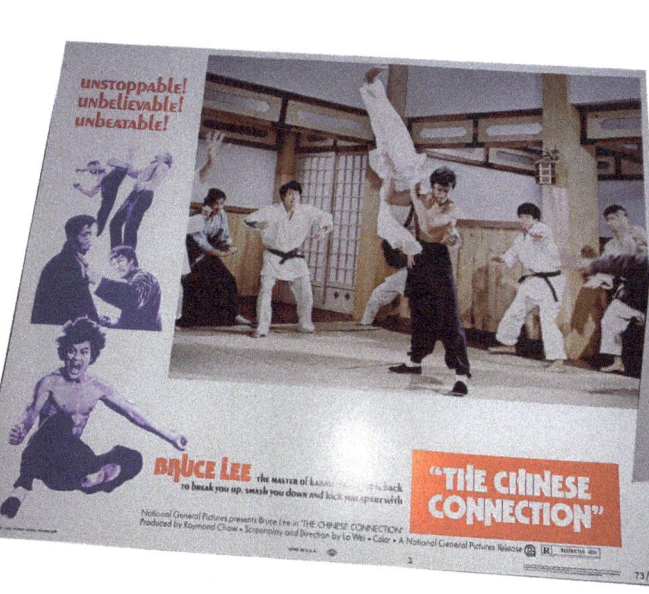

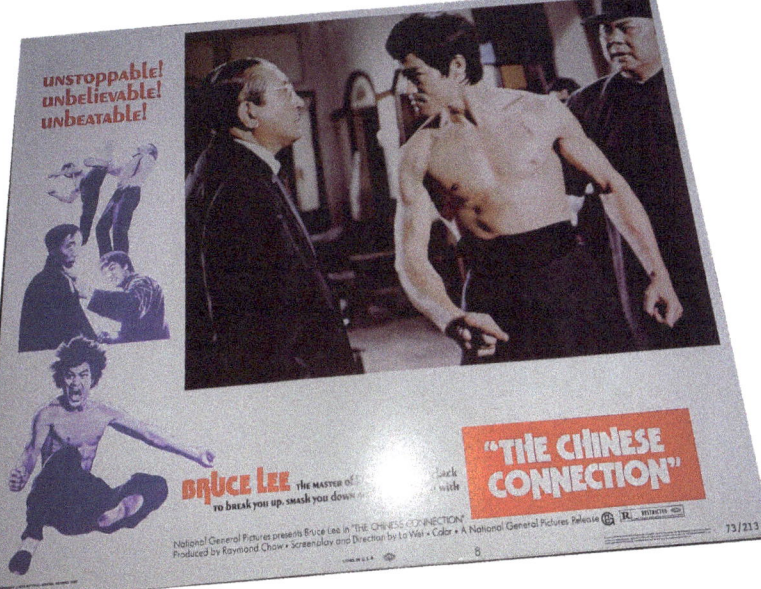

BRUCE'S SINGING RODS OF IRON

56 *Fist of Fury* Photographic Collection Vol. 2

JAPAN'S BRUCE LEE FEVER
TSUYOSHI IMAI

The Bruce Lee whirlwind, which began with "Enter the Dragon" released in Japan in December 1973, continued in 1974. In the spring of that year, the long-awaited second *The Big Boss* was released, and the Bruce Lee boom is finally heading to the climax. Yes, on July 20, 1974, the anniversary of Bruce Lee's death, the third *Fist of Fury* was finally released. At the height of the boom, all over Japan has come to Bruce Lee's fever rather than the summer heat. Bruce Lee's trademark nunchaku and cry of fight can be enjoyed to the fullest. I was so excited by the theme song of the record that I listened to repeatedly before the release, and I was finally knocked out by Bruce Lee and by the beautiful Nora Miao.

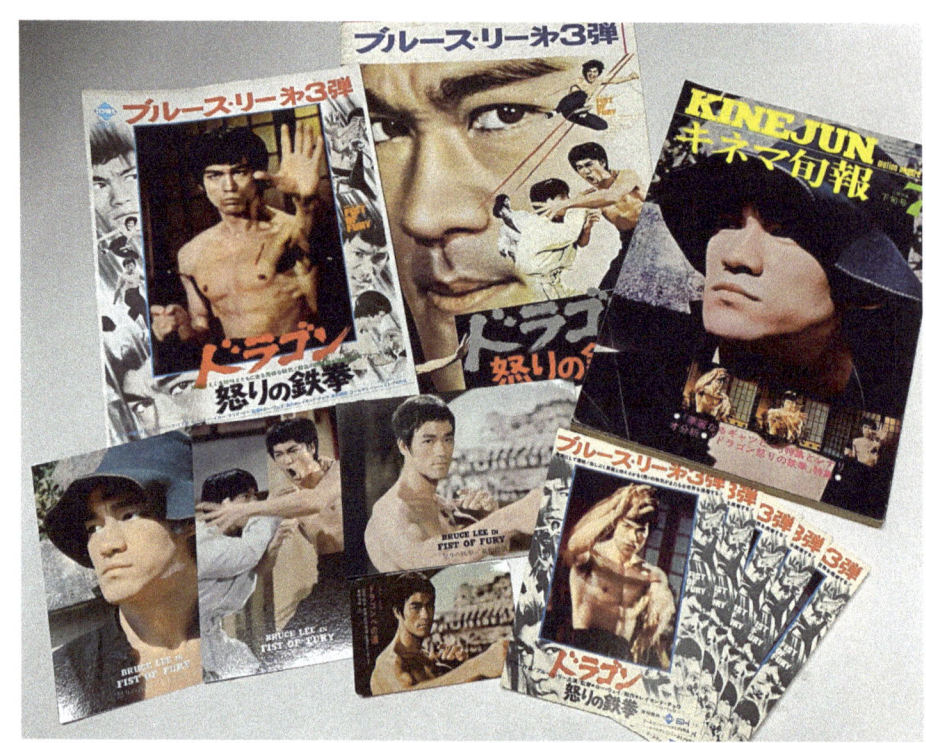

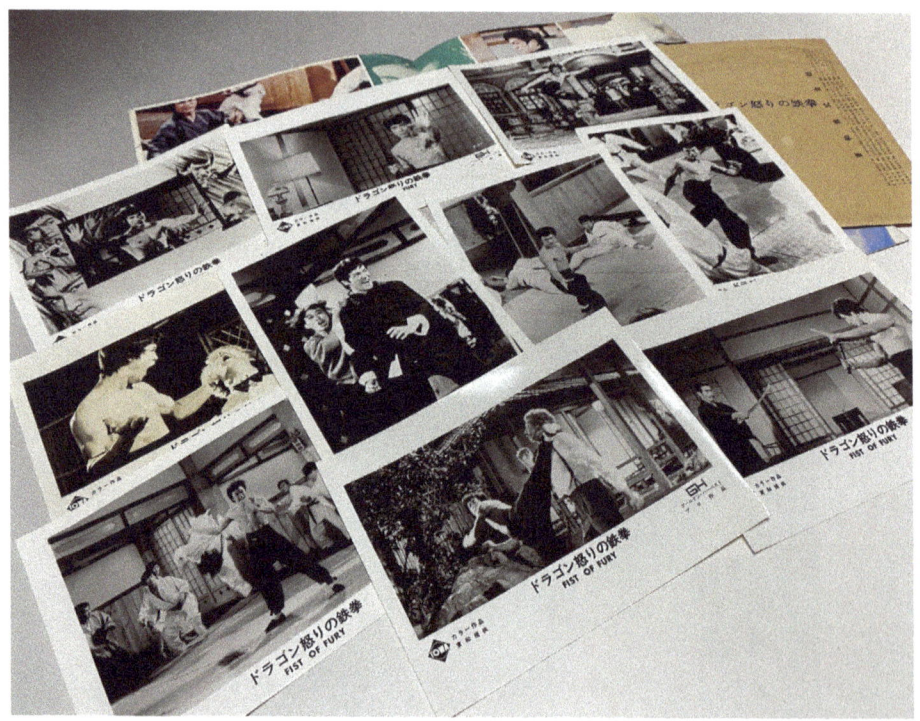

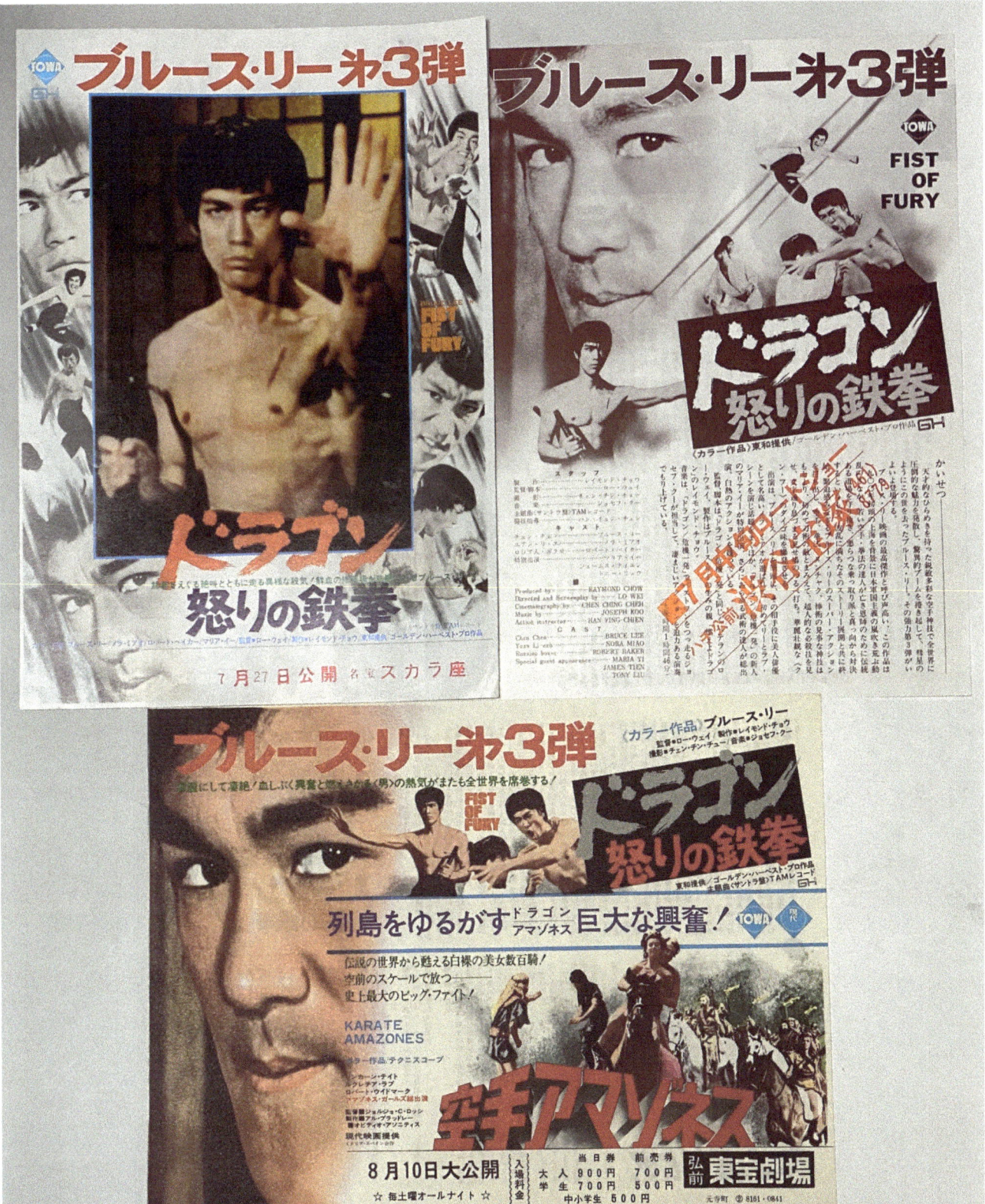

"WE ARE NOT SICK MEN OF ASIA"

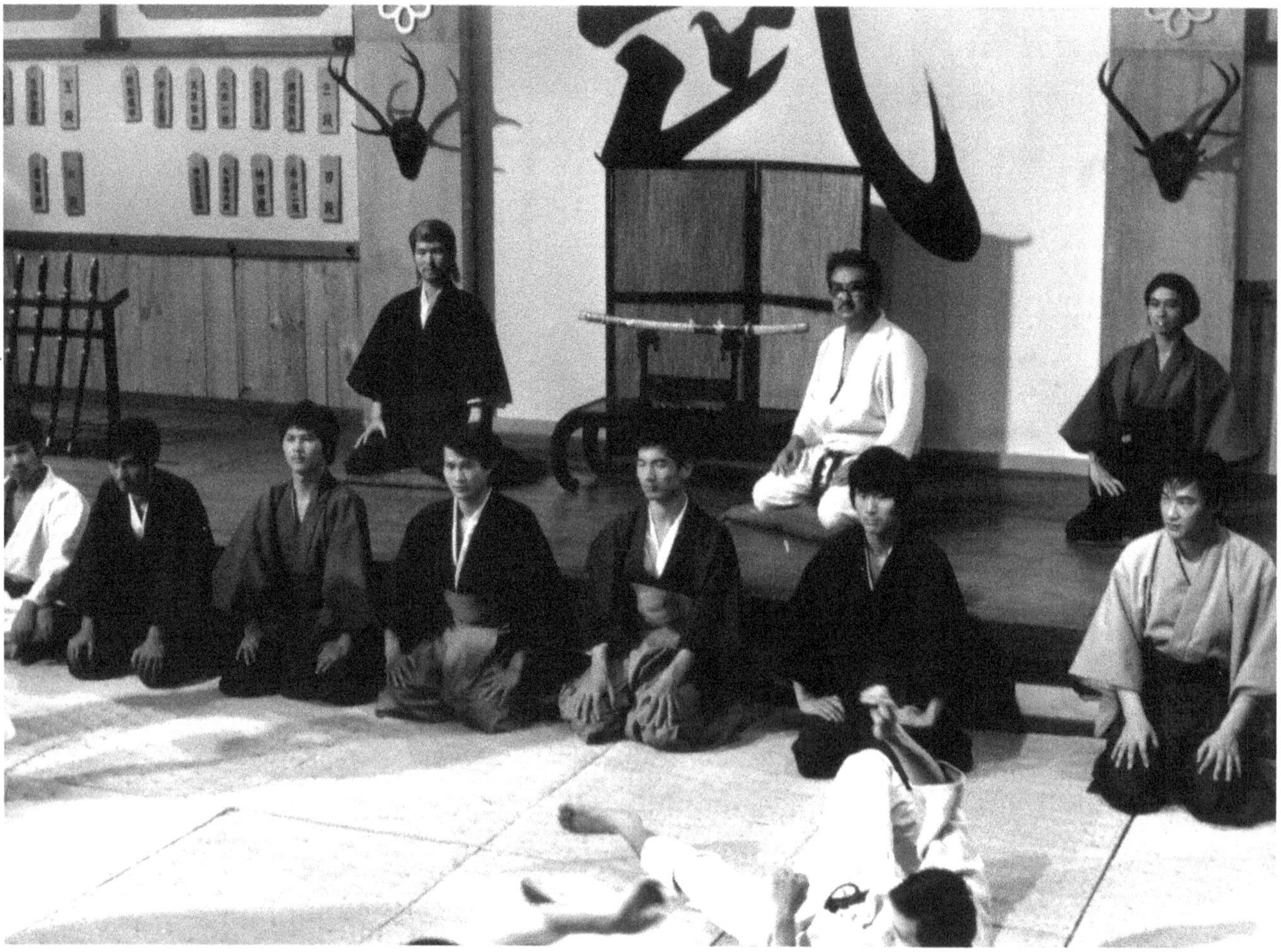

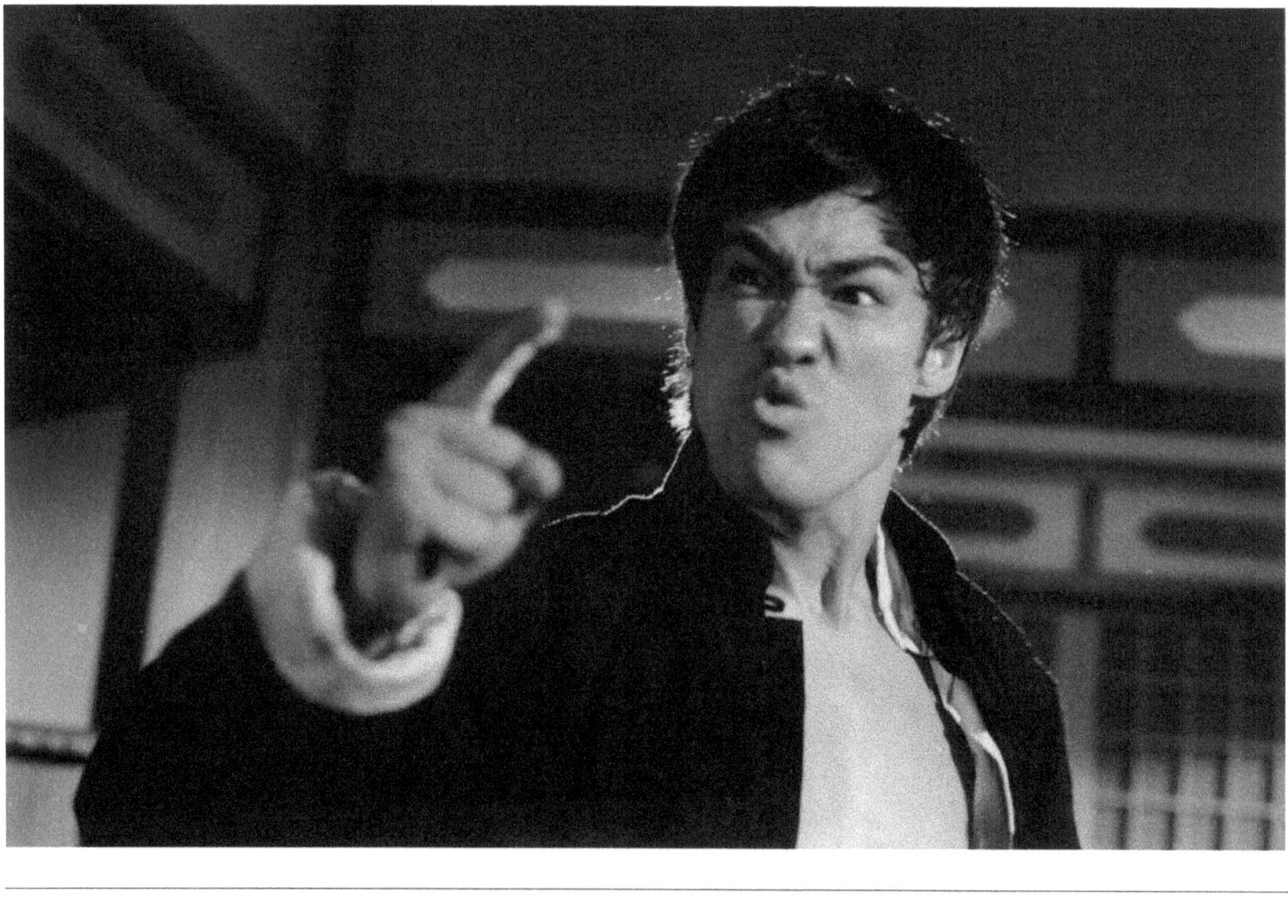

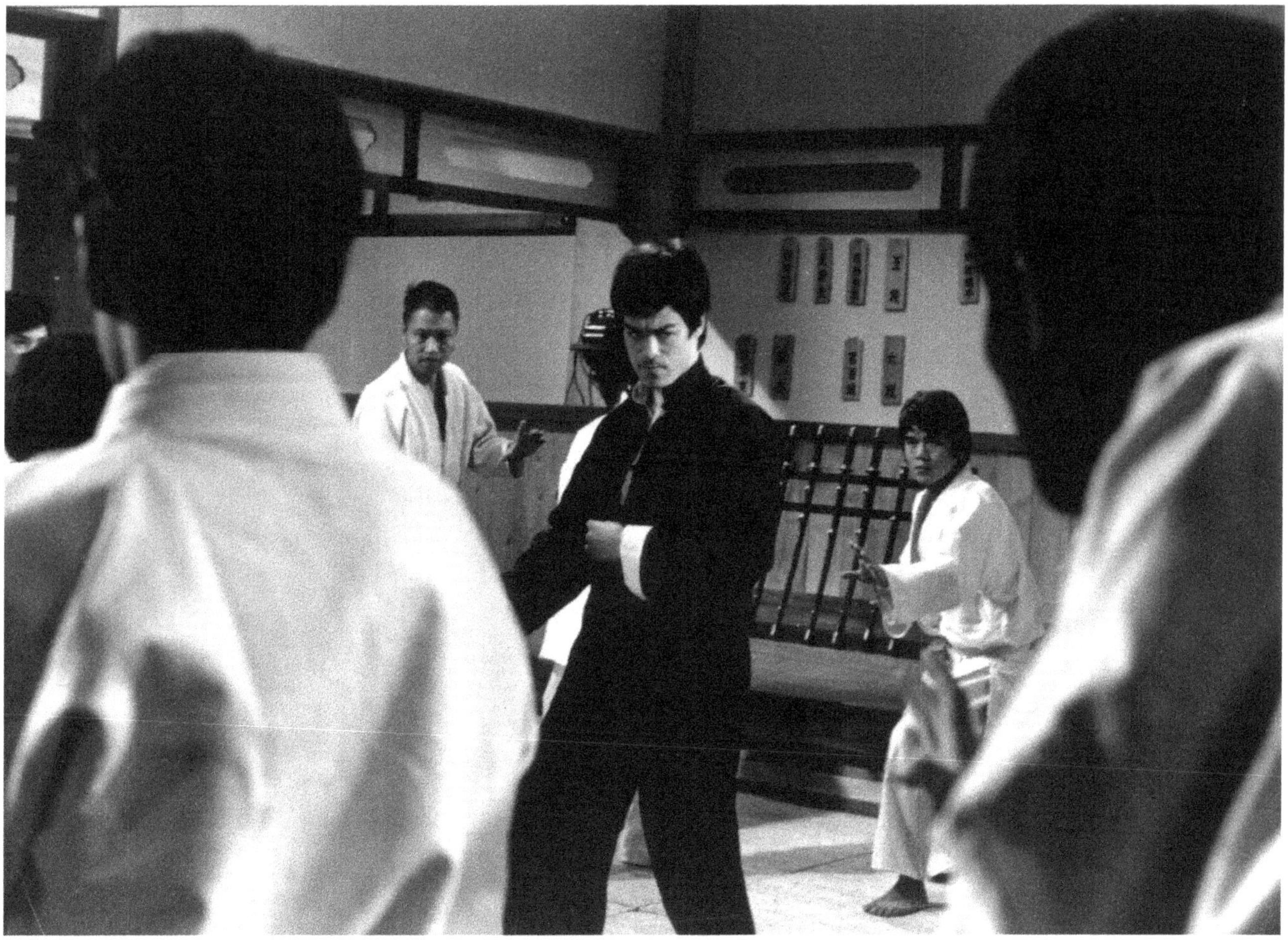

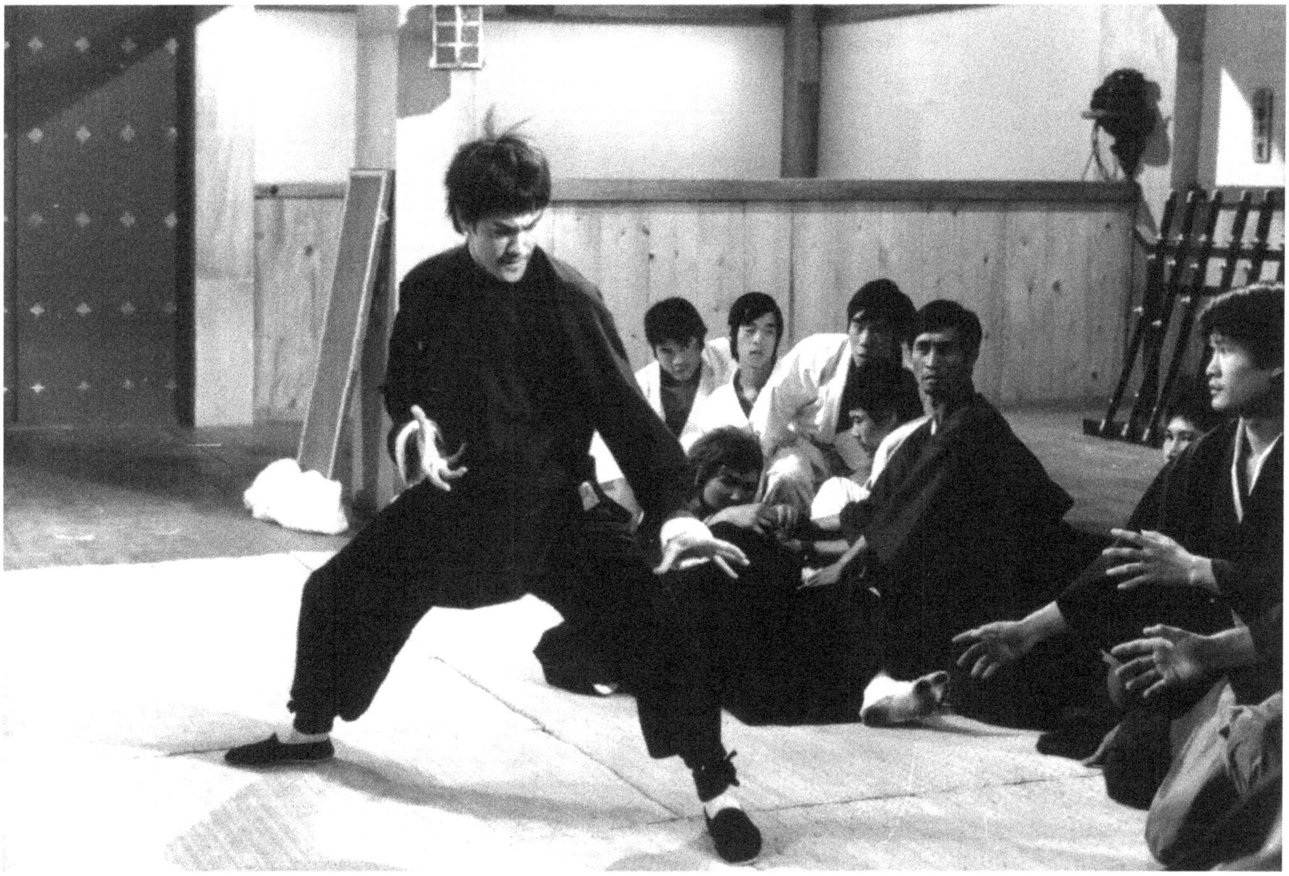

Fist of Fury Photographic Collection Vol. 2

70 *Fist of Fury* Photographic Collection Vol. 2

Fist of Fury Photographic Collection Vol. 2

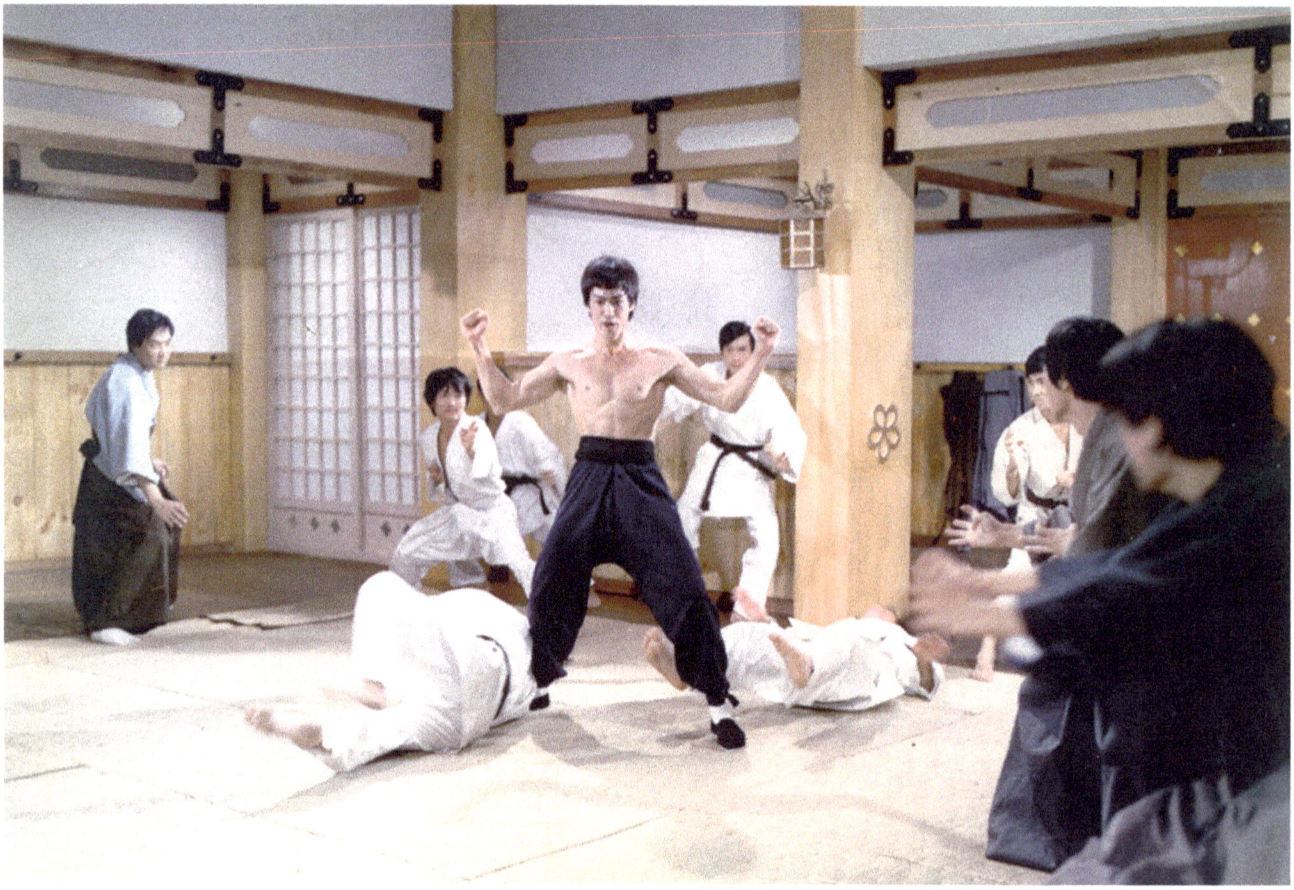

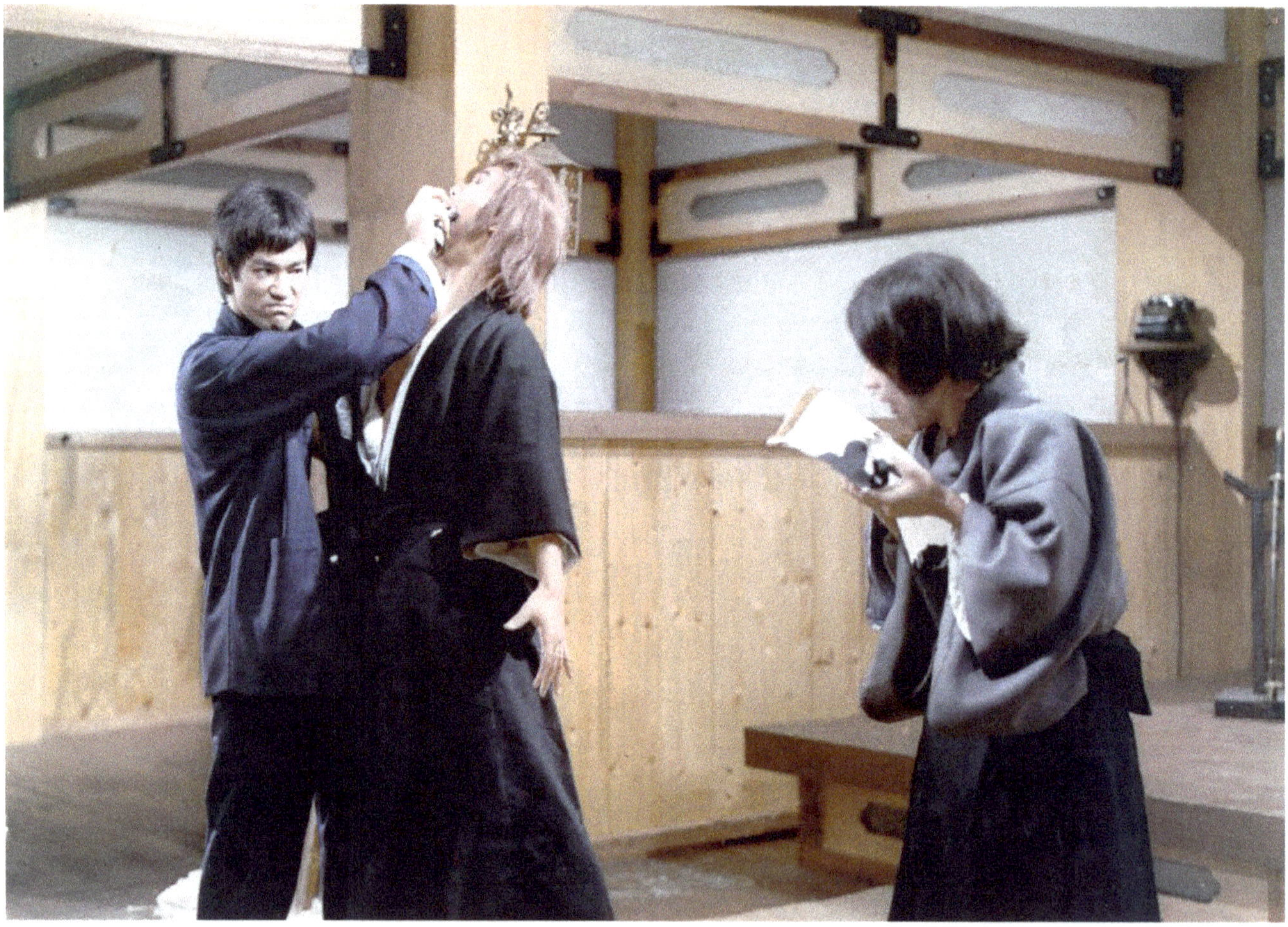

Fist of Fury Photographic Collection Vol. 2　　73

THE FINAL CONFRONTATION

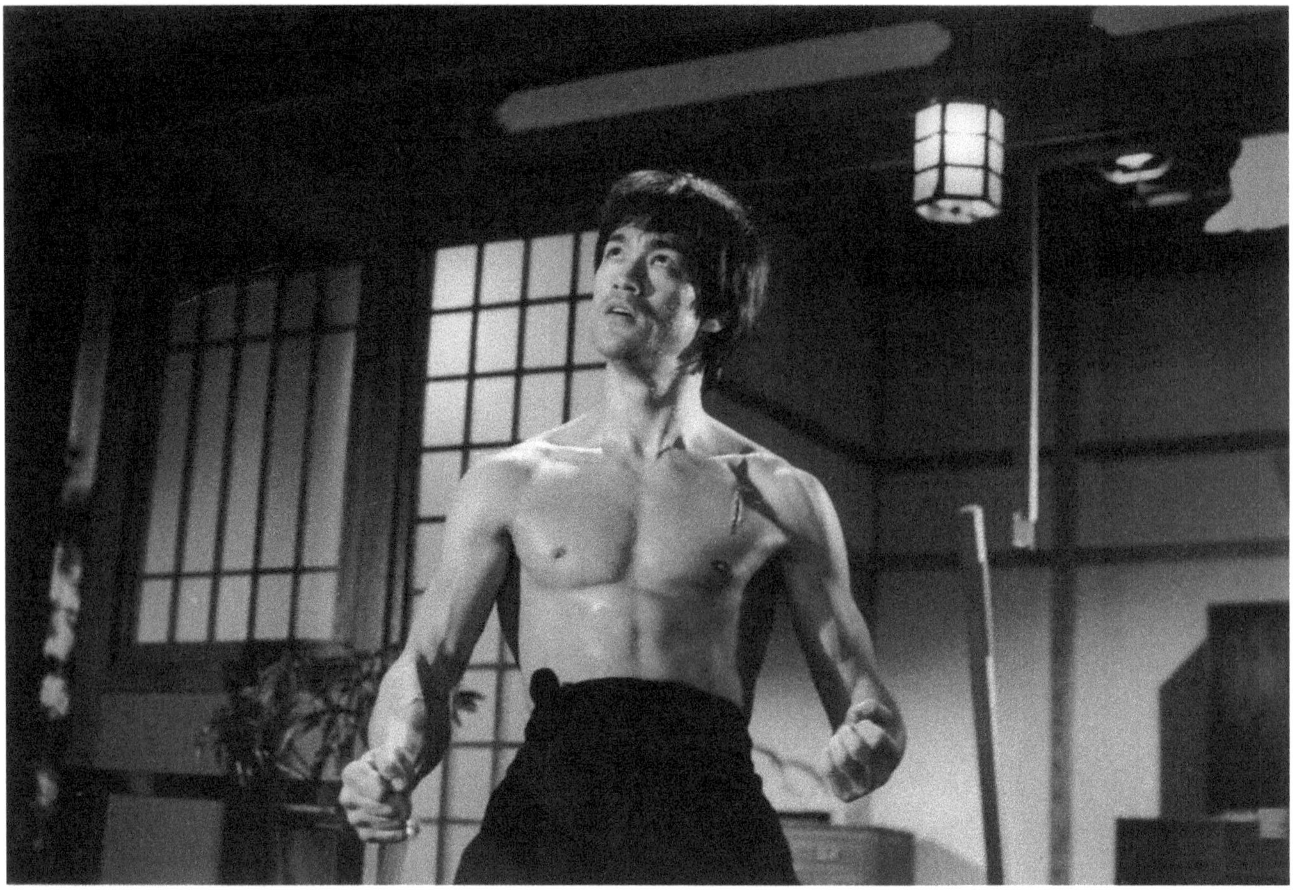

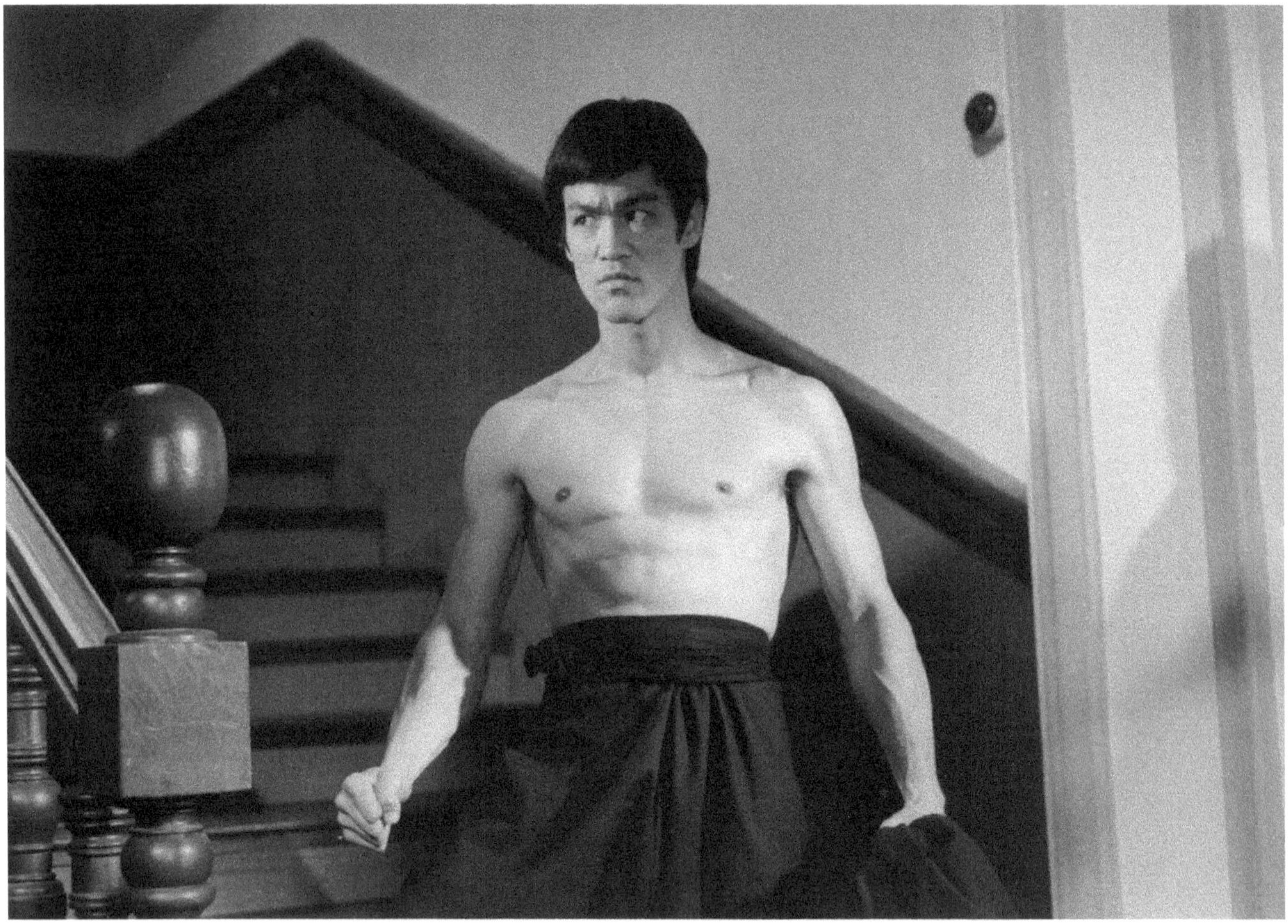

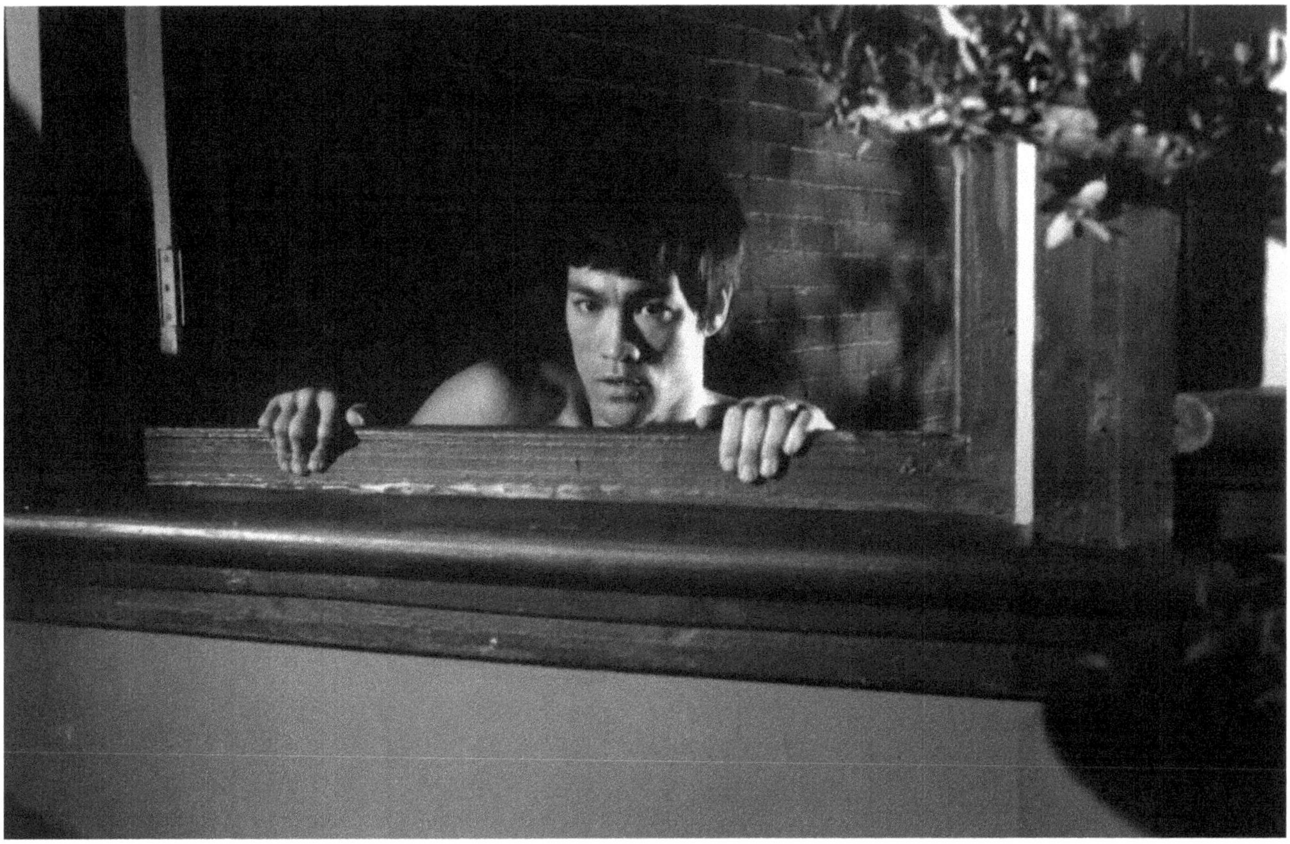

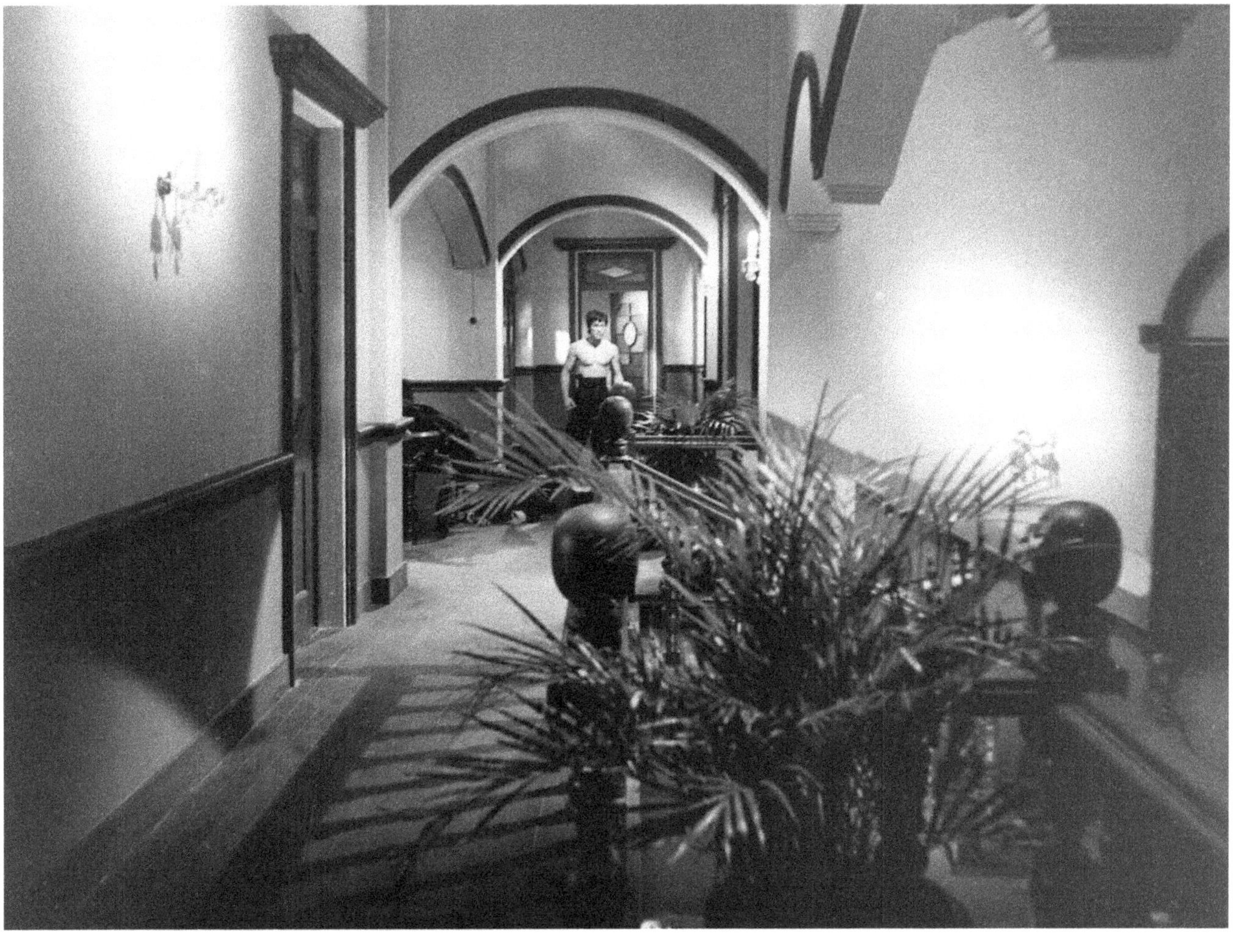

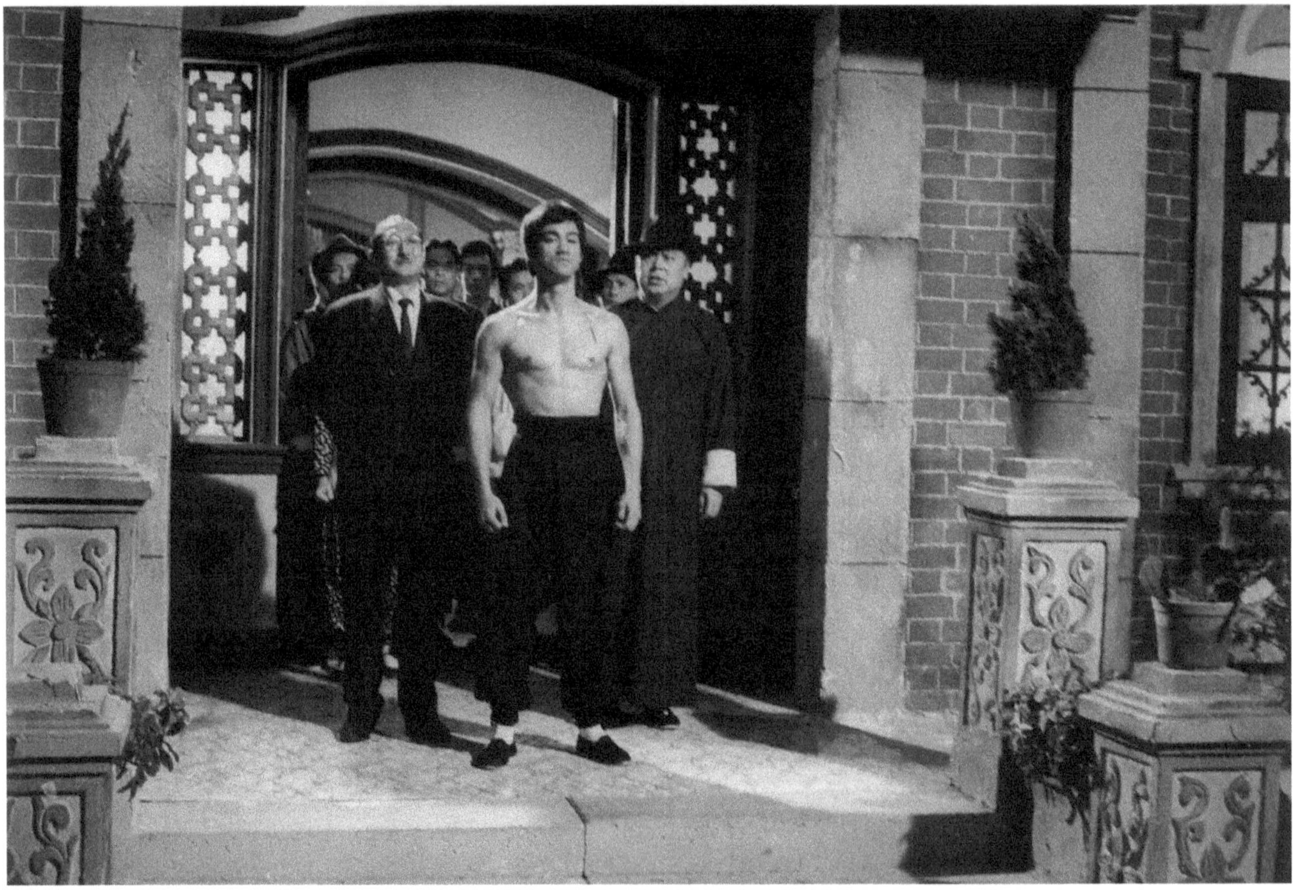

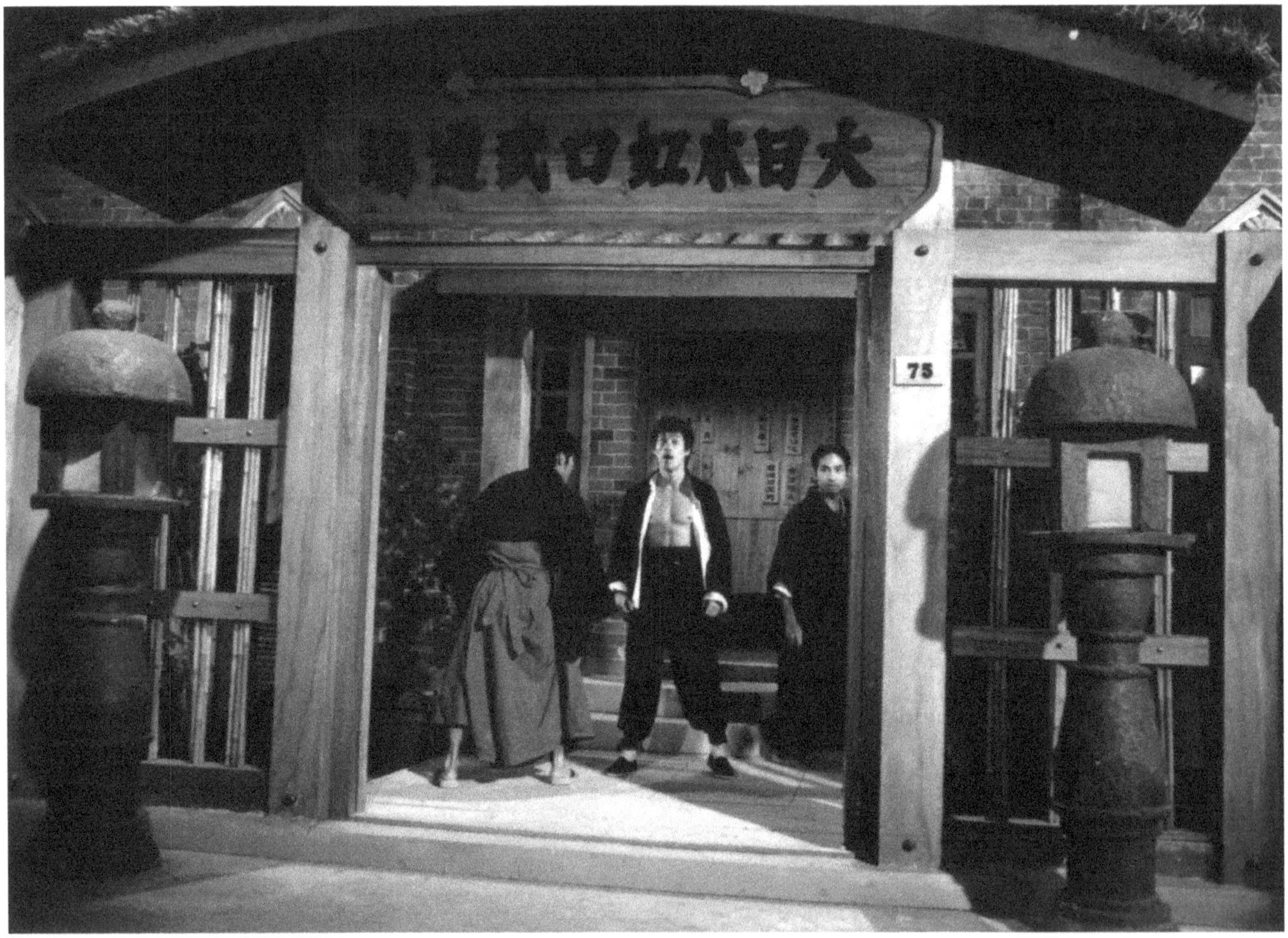
大日本虹口武道
75

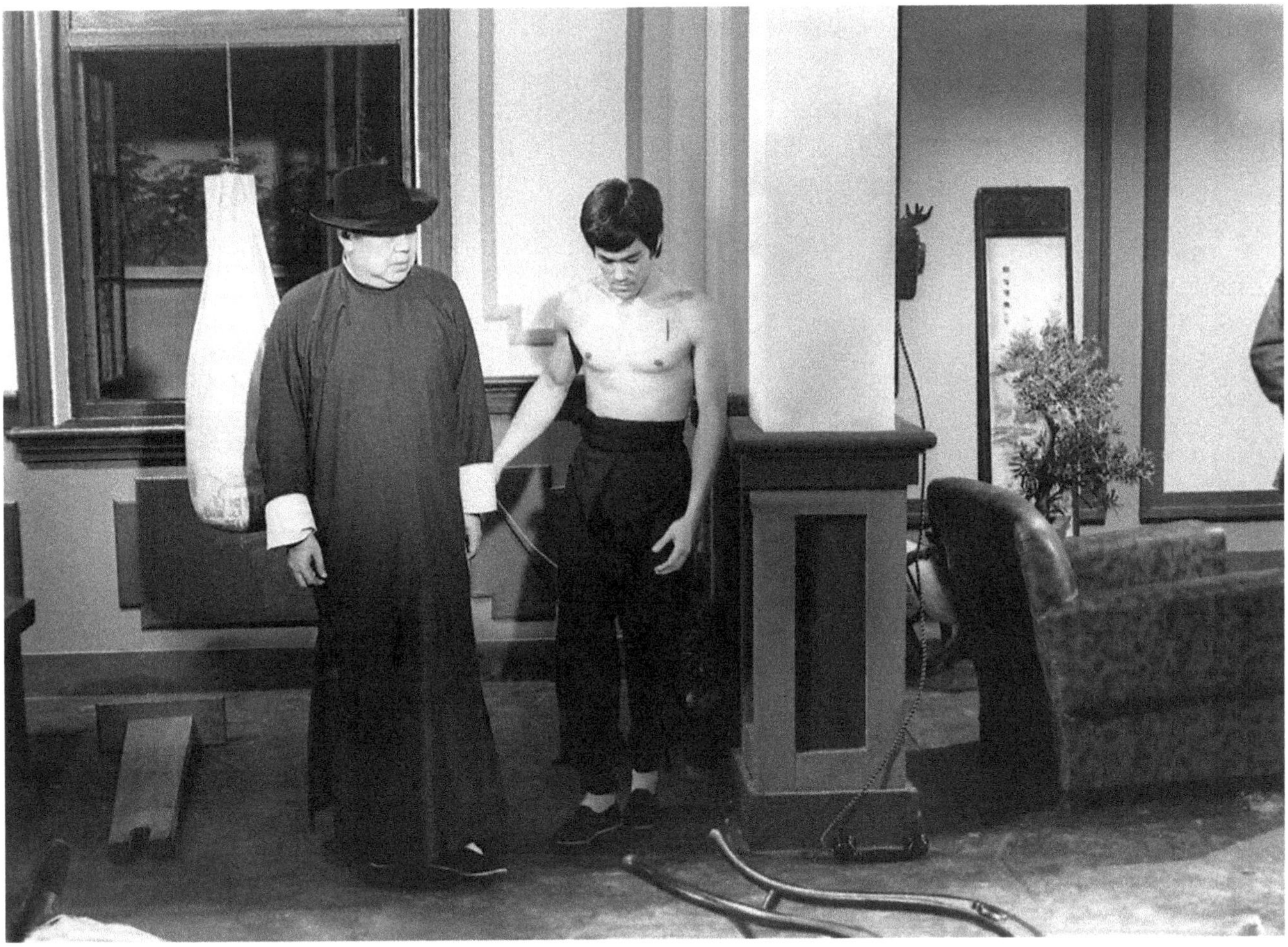

Fist of Fury Photographic Collection Vol. 2

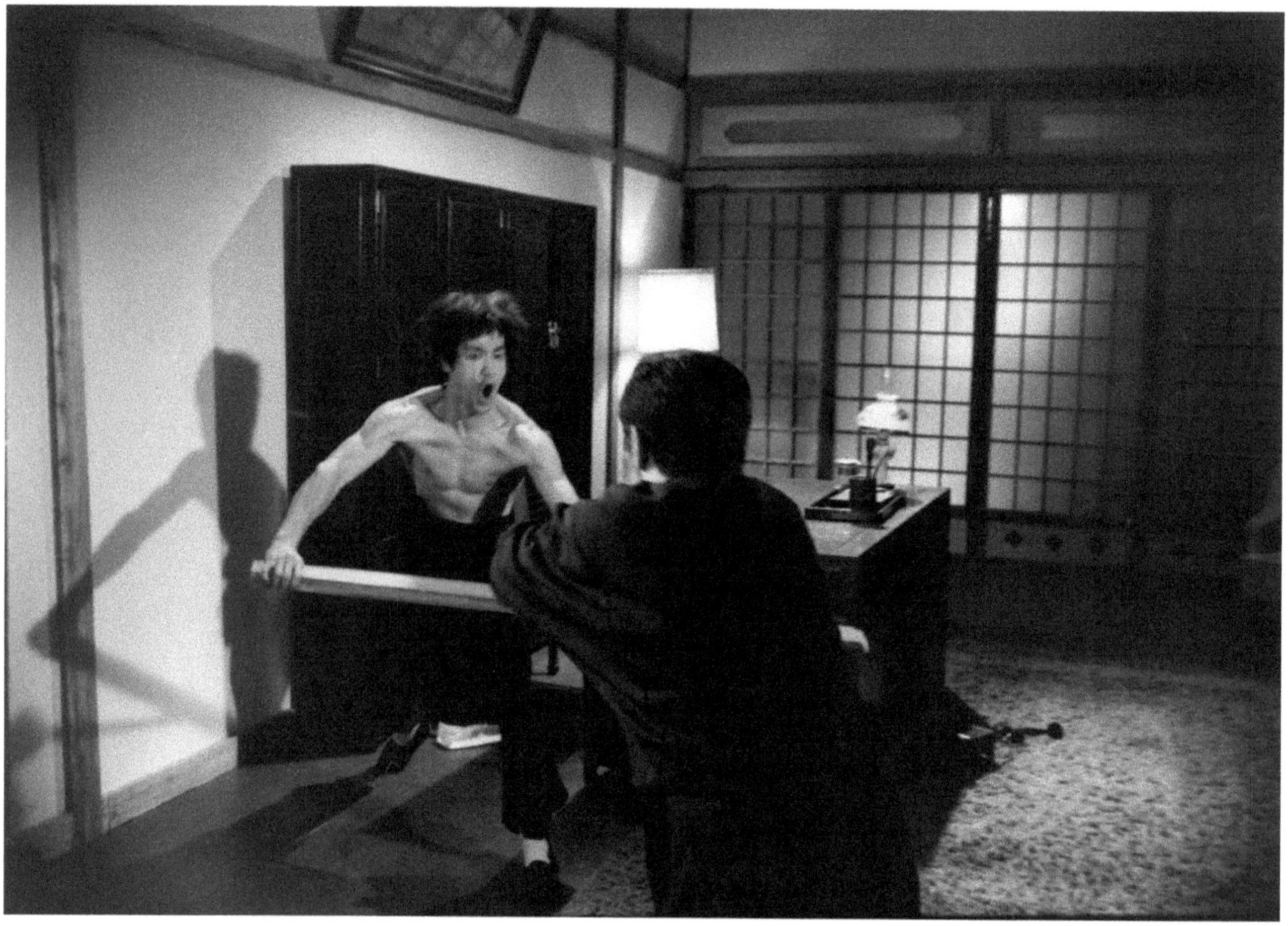

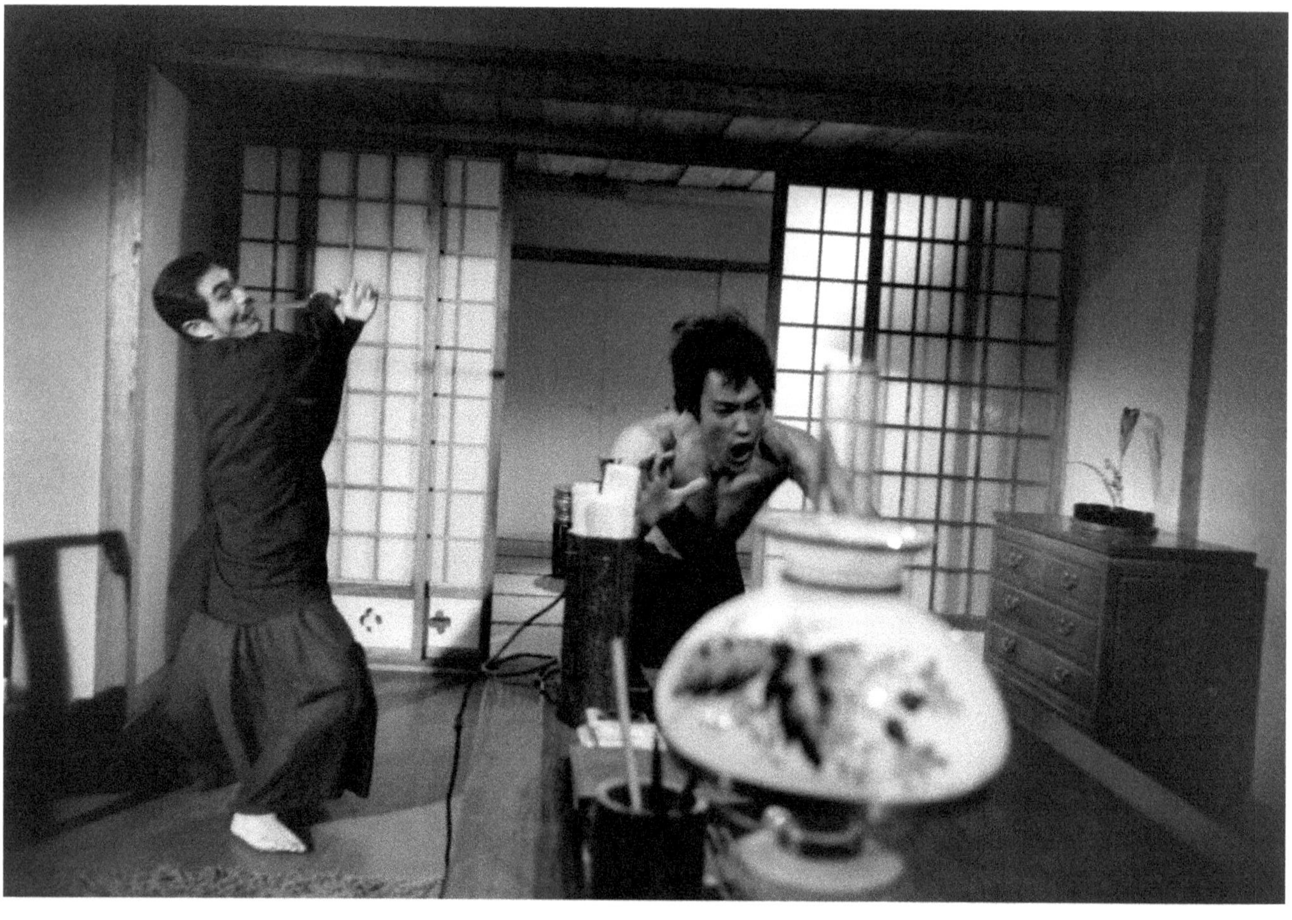

Fist of Fury Photographic Collection Vol. 2

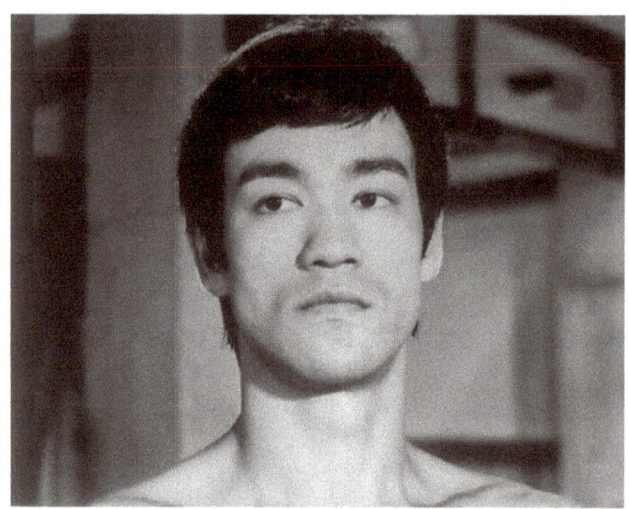

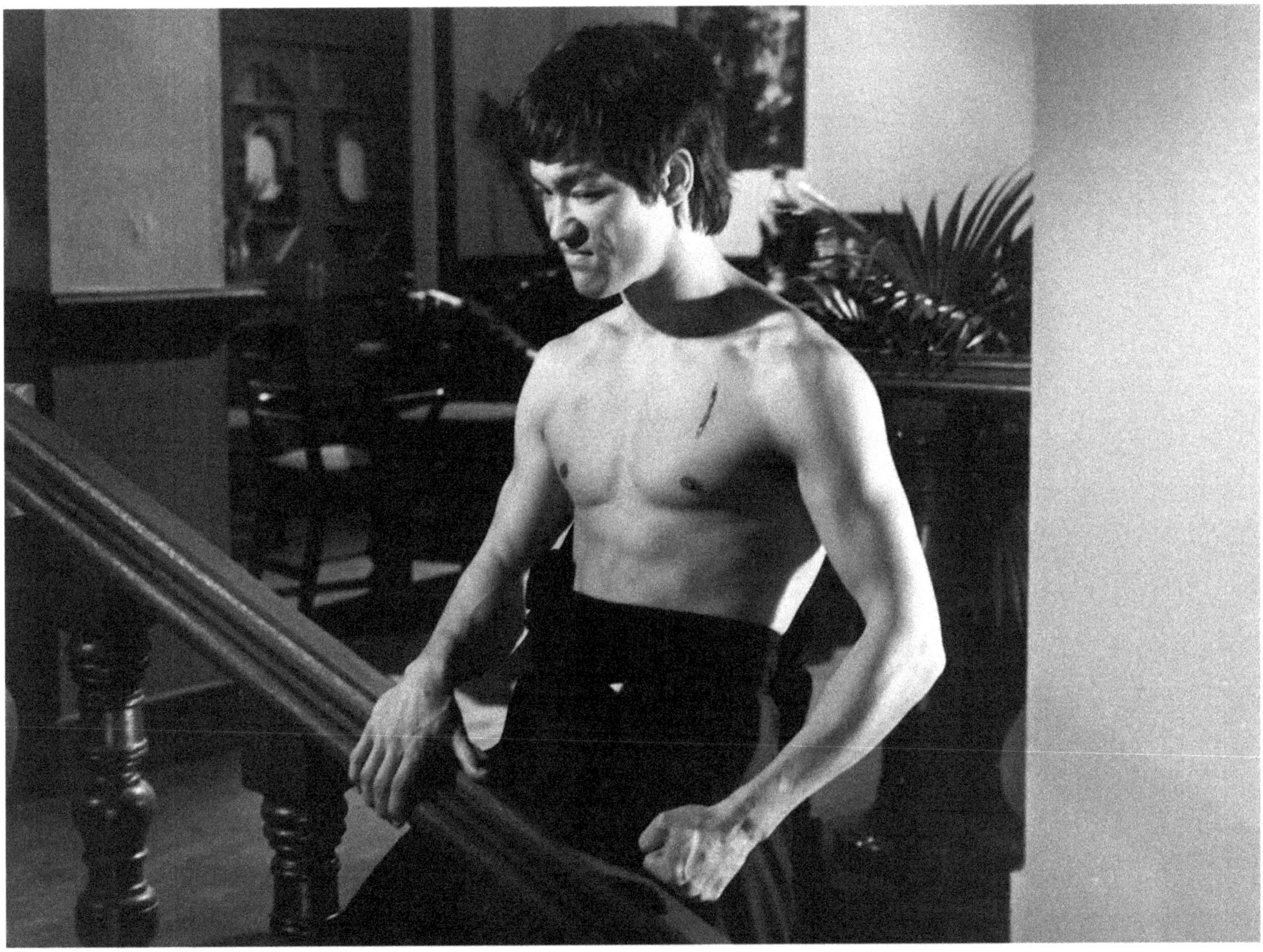

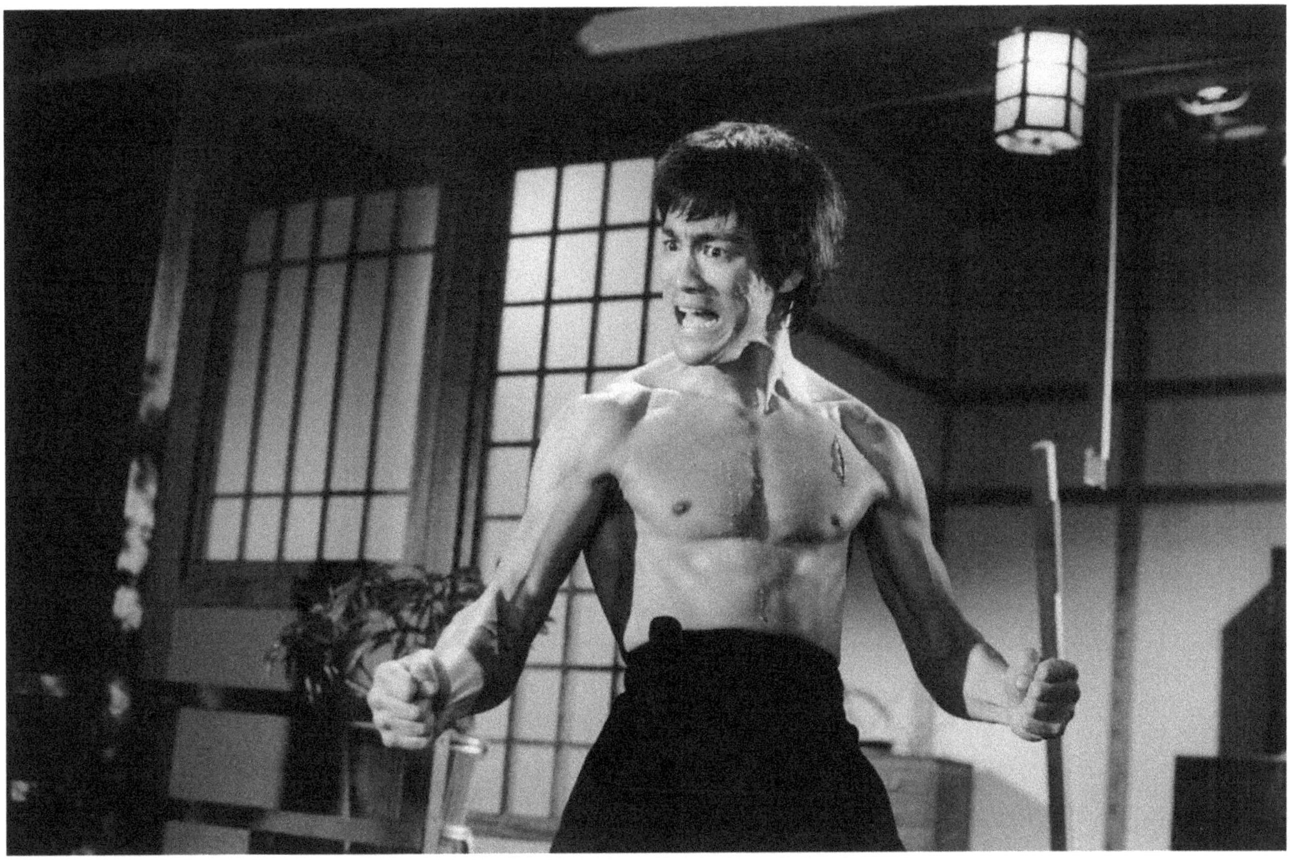

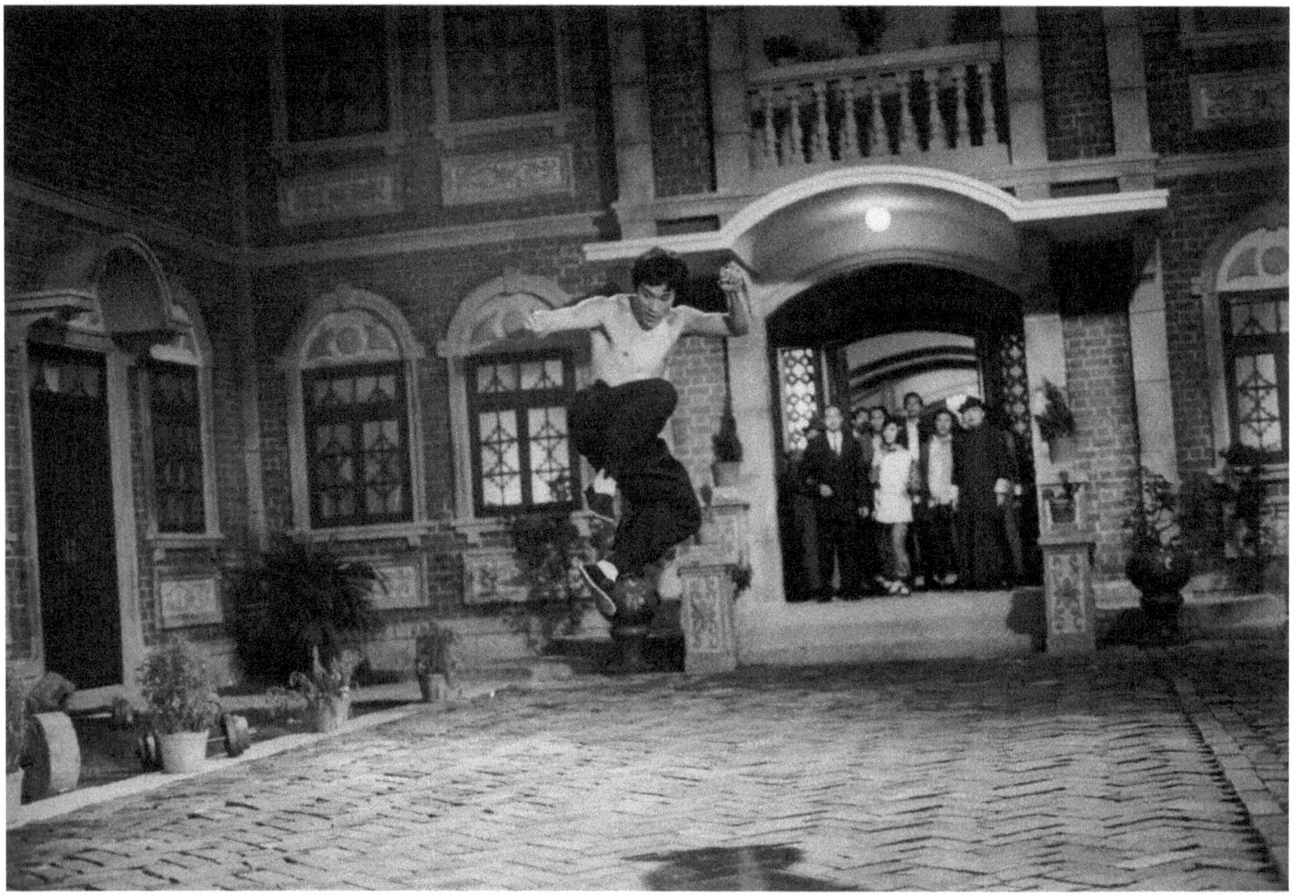

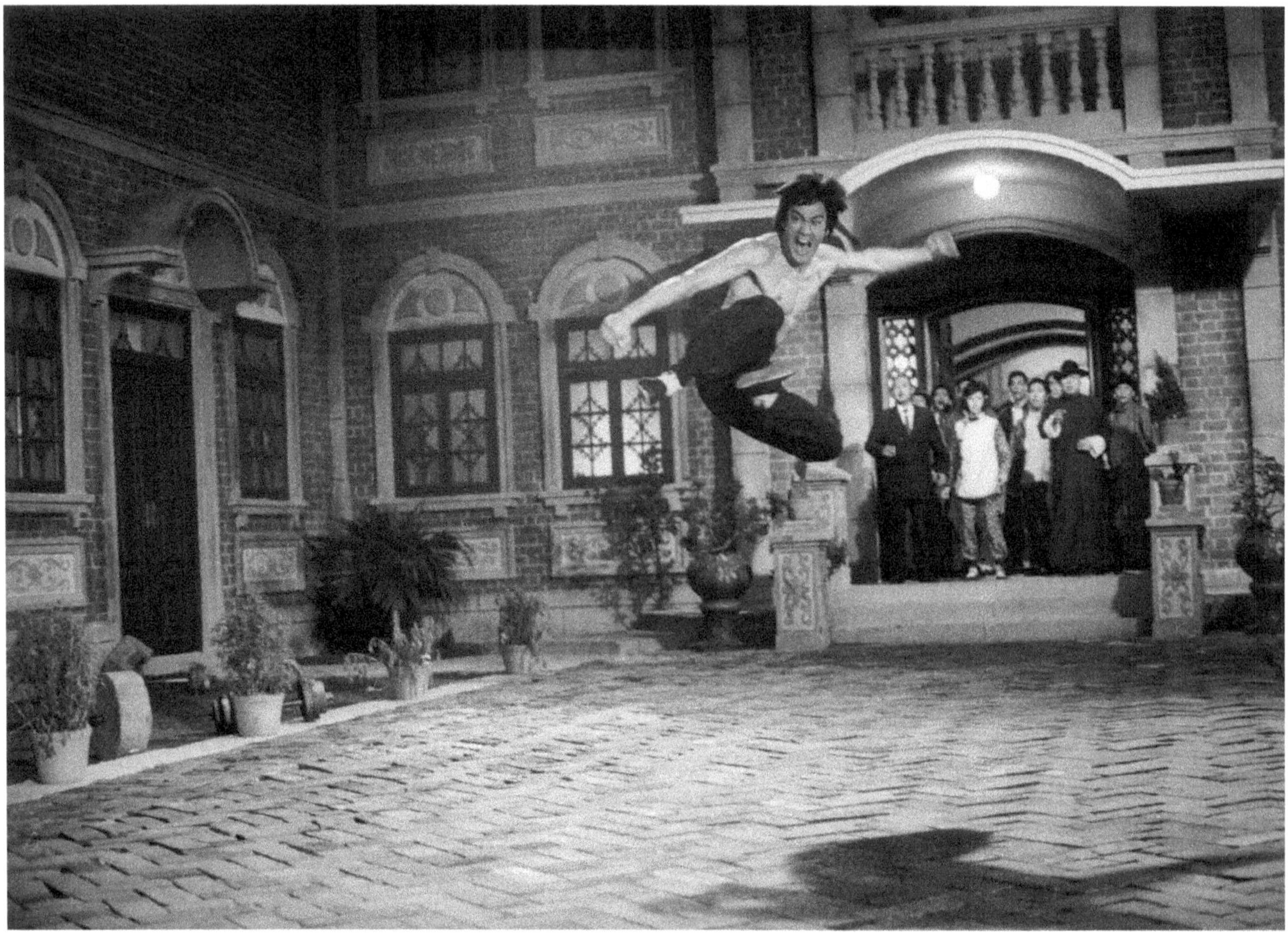

BEHIND THE SCENES

Fist of Fury Photographic Collection Vol. 2

92   *Fist of Fury* Photographic Collection Vol. 2

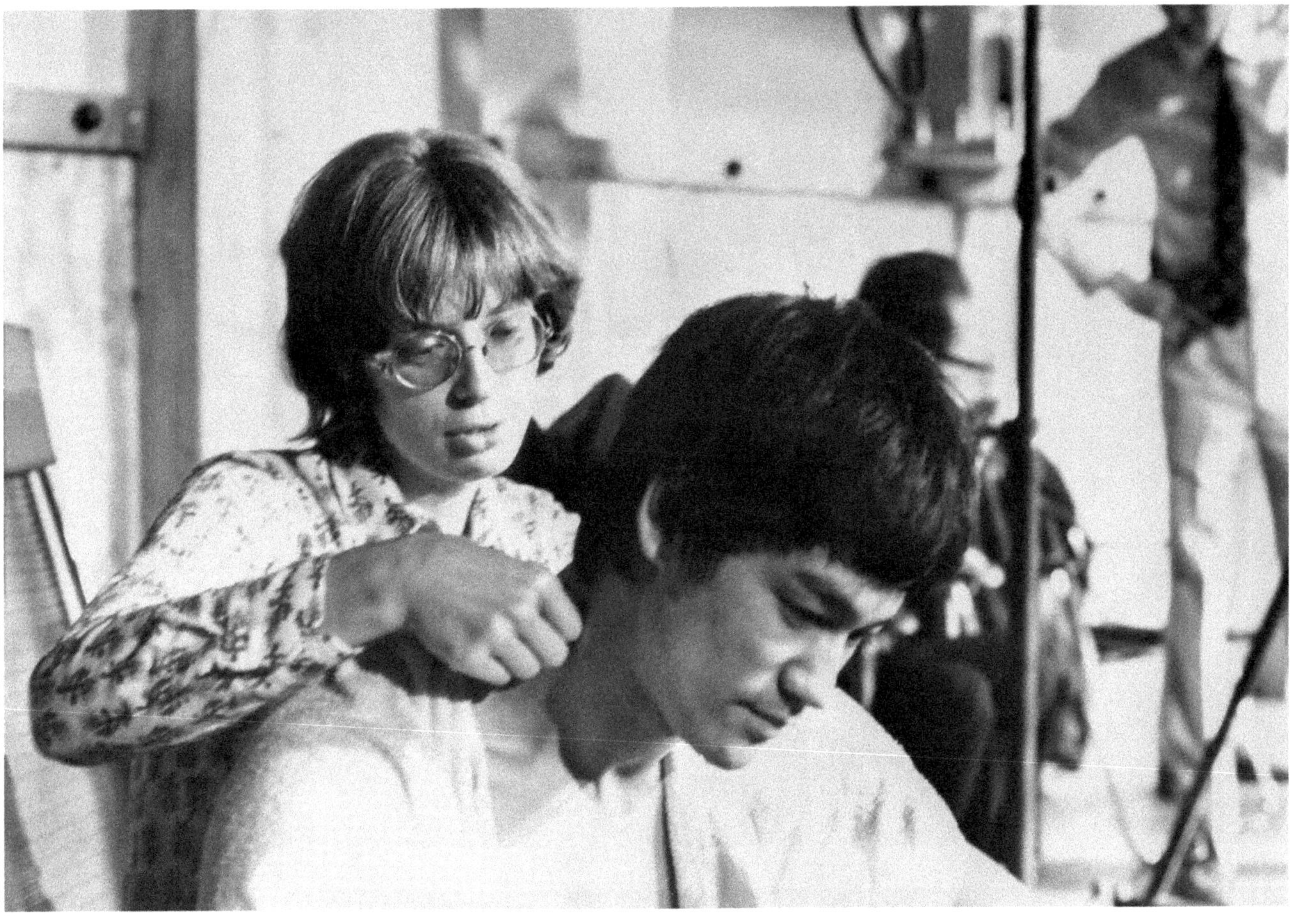

Fist of Fury Photographic Collection Vol. 2

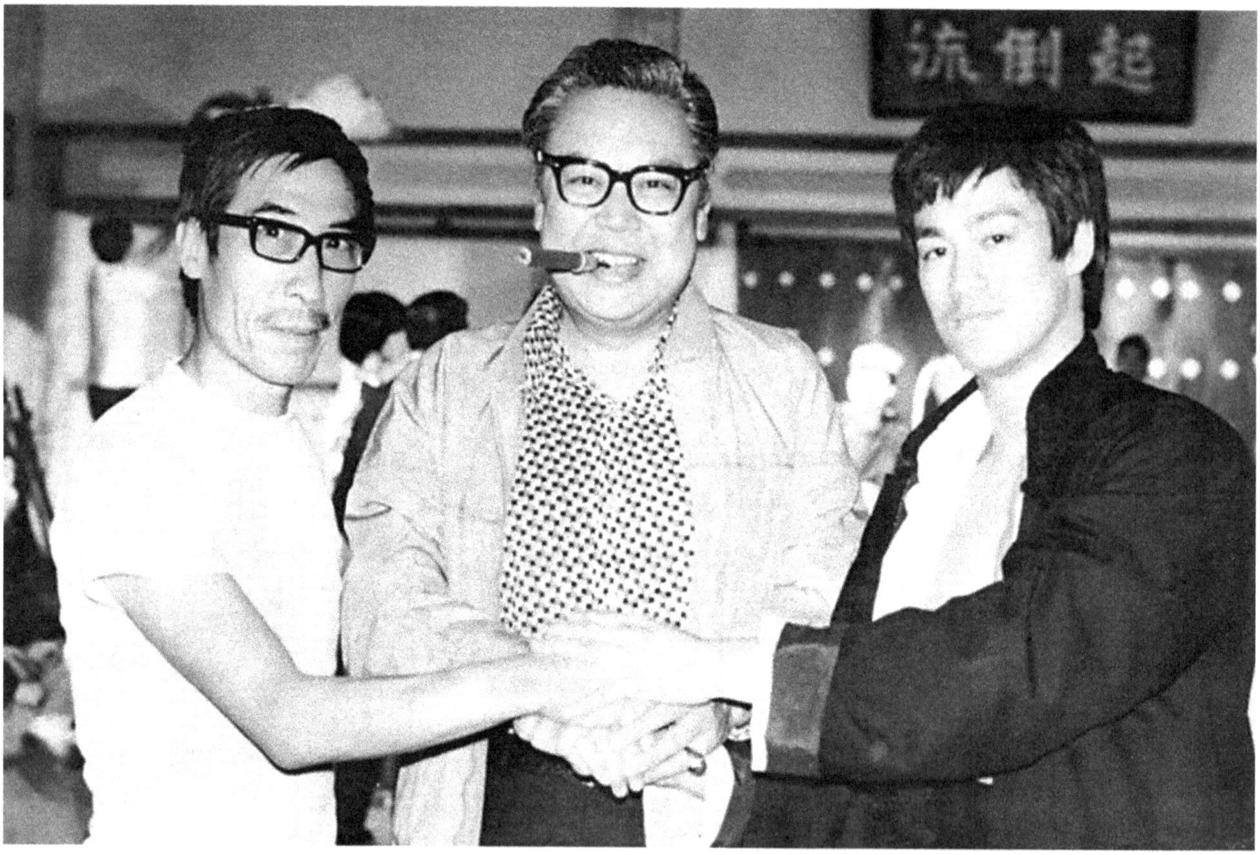

94 *Fist of Fury* Photographic Collection Vol. 2

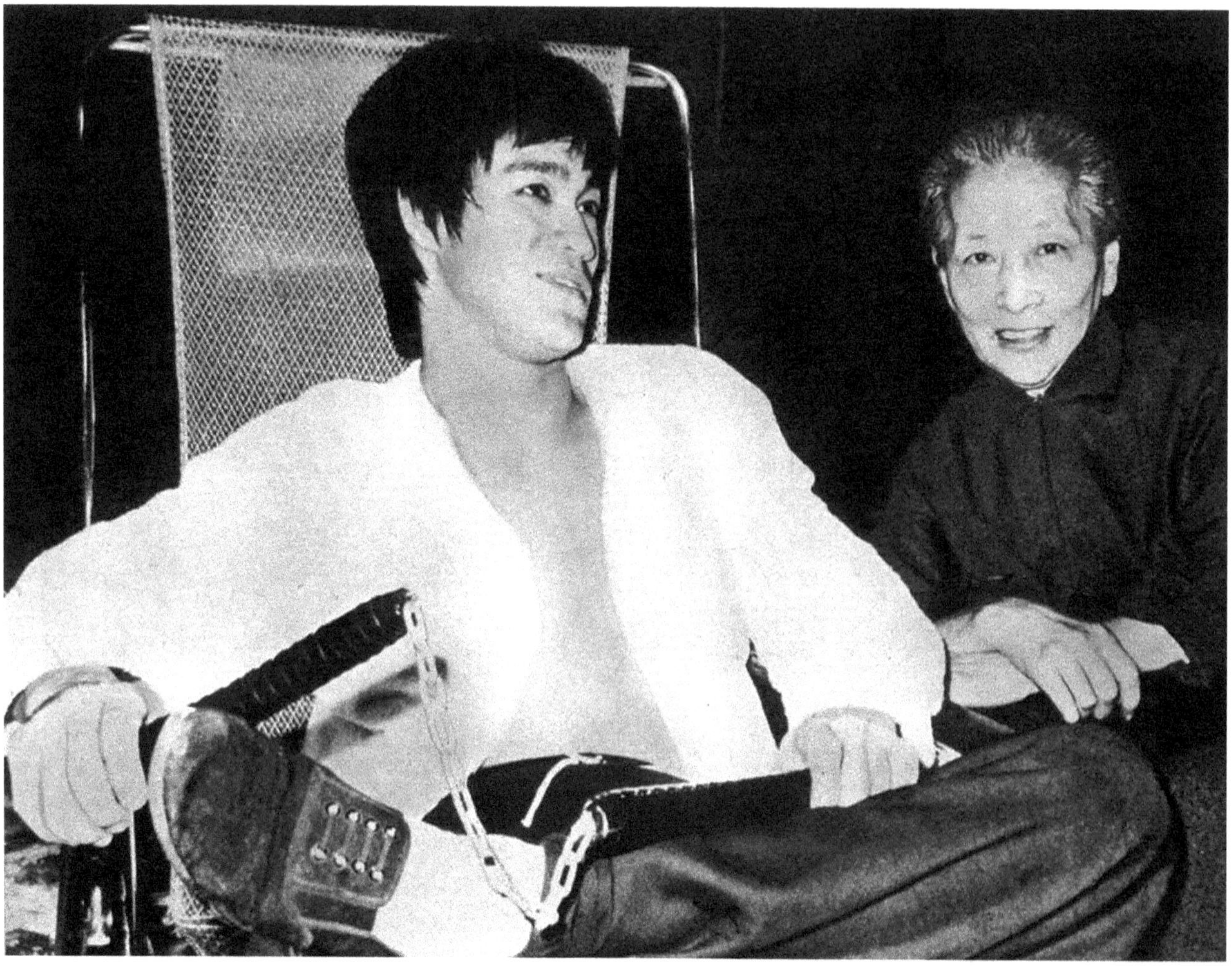

Fist of Fury Photographic Collection Vol. 2

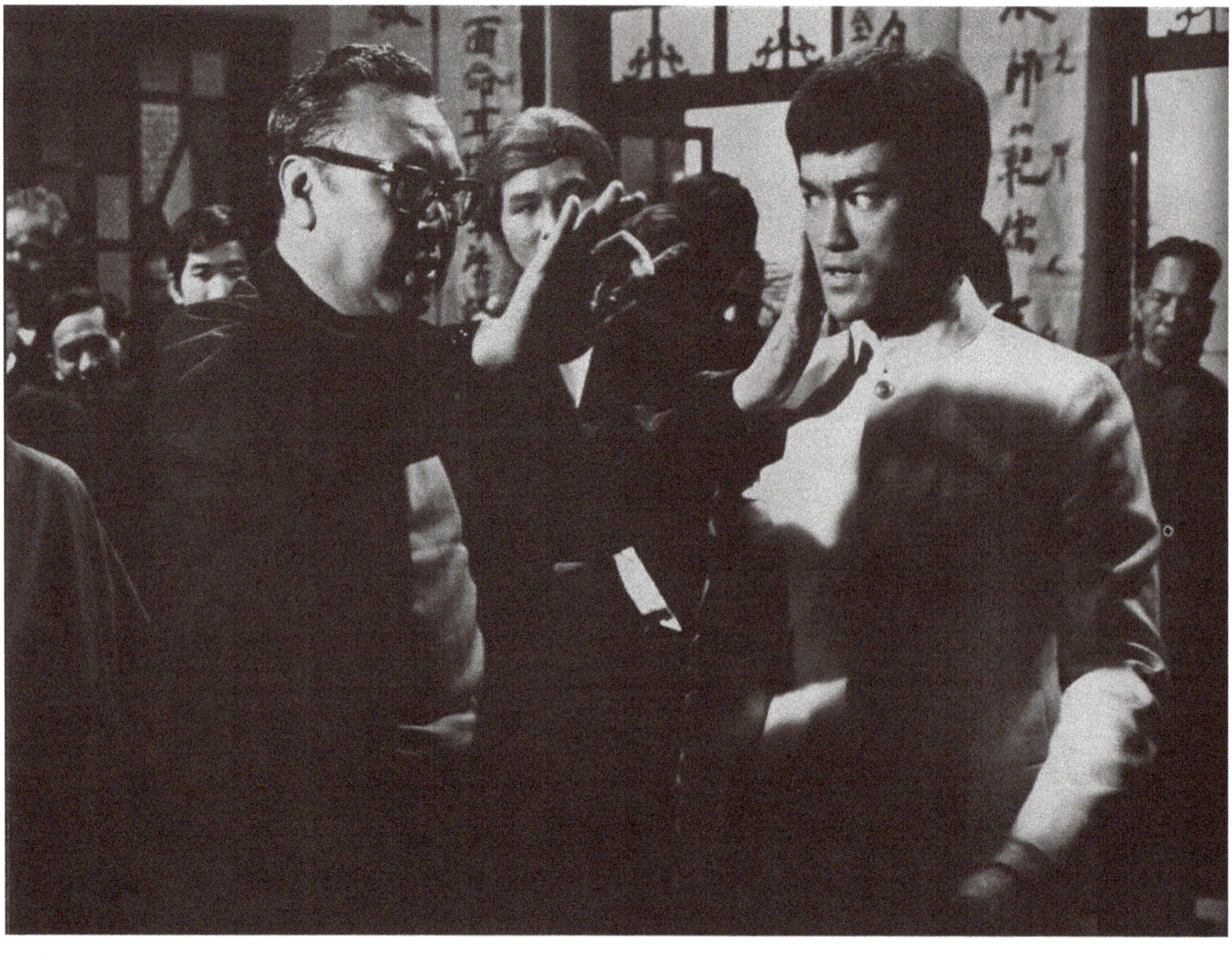

Fist of Fury Photographic Collection Vol. 2

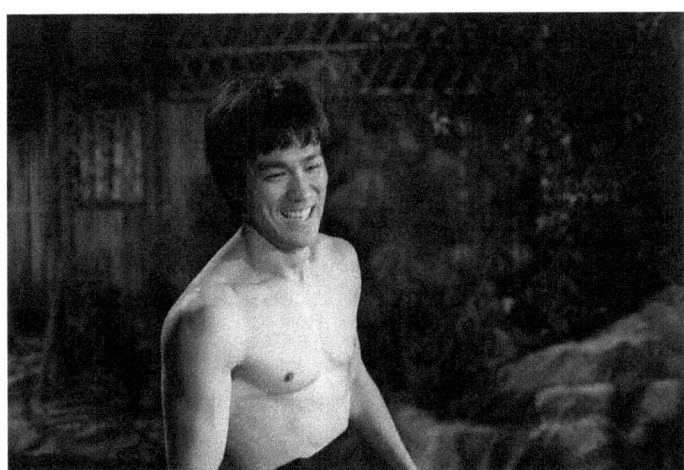

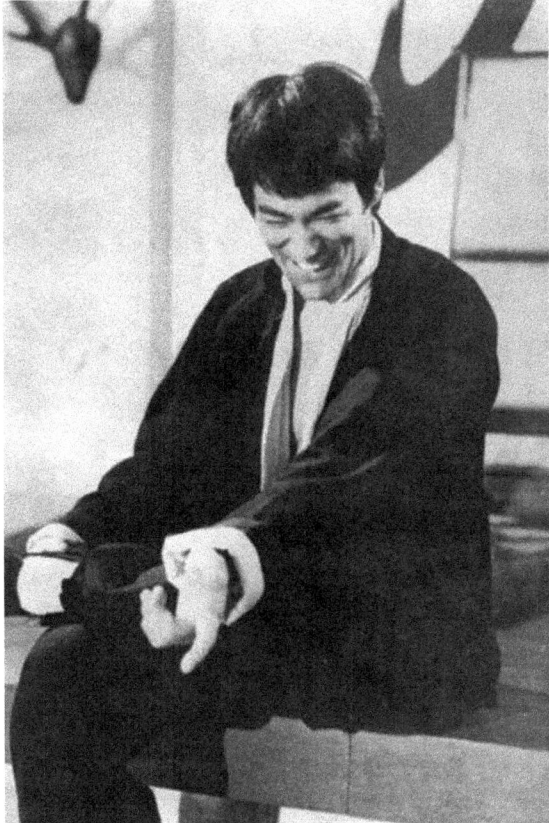